AMERICAN
PRIDE

AMERICAN PRIDE

DIANA ROSEN

CITADEL PRESS
Kensington Publishing Corp.
www.kensingtonbooks.com

CITADEL PRESS books are published by

Kensington Publishing Corp.
850 Third Avenue
New York, NY 10022

Permission to reprint "The Americans (A Canadian's Opinion)," © 1973, Newstalk Radio CFRB AM 1010, Toronto, Canada, is gratefully acknowledged.

All Kensington titles, imprints, and distributed lines are available at special quantity discounts for bulk purchases for sales promotions, premiums, fund raising, educational, or institutional use. Special book excerpts or customized printings can also be created to fit specific needs. For details, write or phone the office of the Kensington special sales manager: Kensington Publishing Corp., 850 Third Avenue, New York, NY 10022, attn: Special Sales Department, phone 1-800-221-2647.

Citadel Press and the Citadel logo are trademarks of Kensington Publishing Corp.

First printing: November 2001

10 9 8 7 6 5 4 3

Printed in the United States of America

Preassigned Control Number (PCN) may be obtained from the Library of Congress.

ISBN 0-8065-2394-8

Dedicated
to
"We the People"

The cause of America is in a great measure the cause of all mankind …

—Thomas Paine
Common Sense, 1776

CONTENTS

PREFACE

Dear Fellow Americans:

We've been challenged, you and I: on our doorstep, in our hearts, in our minds. This book, in part, is an answer to that challenge.

We've been attacked by people who fear our freedoms and our success; criticized by others too selfish to contribute to our defense and without memory of our past generosity to them.

This book asks, "What can Americans be proud of?" and it answers with so many exemplary historical highlights and cultural contributions that we had to leave out enough additional material for several other books.

During the aftermath of the events of September 11, 2001, we quickly learned that we are more than our skin color, greater than our religious beliefs or our ancestral heritage, beyond the differences of political opinions or the many differences among service people and professionals, farmers and teachers, laborers and artists: *We are all Americans and we are in this together.*

All of us are grateful that we have the best equipped, best trained, best strategic defense forces in the world; we have the most responsive, most innovative municipal disaster and crisis teams, unequaled in any other nation; we are honored to have friends and neighbors who show up to donate blood, work where needed, give money and food—without being asked. We are proud of them.

We are Americans. We can choose how to make and spend our money, choose how to live our lives, and choose how to vote.

We can choose to drive a pickup truck or a family sedan; choose grits and eggs, caviar on toast, or a tossed salad, hold the dressing. We can paint our nails, pierce body parts, or let the hair go gray. We can party or we can pray, we can be hermits or social animals; we can travel the world or never leave home, sample several careers or stay in one field for thirty years.

We love, we laugh, we live knowing we are a nation of the Second Chance, the New Beginning, the Land of Opportunity. Our founding fathers gave us a system of government in which *we* are in charge. We have the right to life, liberty, and the pursuit of happiness.

Turn the page for some of the many reasons to be proud to be an American!

OUR DEMOCRACY

Government is a trust, and the officers of the government are trustees; and both the trust and the trustees are created for the benefit of the people.

—Henry Clay

The Declaration of Independence

We Are a Nation Free From Tyranny

In a letter to his wife dated July 3, 1776, John Adams wrote about the signing of the Declaration of Independence:

Yesterday the greatest question was decided which ever was debated in America; and a greater perhaps never was, now will be, decided among men. A resolution was passed without one dissenting colony, that those United Colonies are, and of right ought to be, free and independent states . . . . The second day of July, 1776, will be the most memorable epoch in the history of America . . . . It ought to be commemorated as the day of deliverance, by solemn acts of devotion to God Almighty. It ought to be solemnized with pomp and parade, with shows, games, sports, guns, bells, bonfires, and illuminations, from one end of this continent to the other, from this time forward for evermore.

Fifty-six men signed the Declaration of Independence, knowing full well that they were risking their property, their freedom, and their lives by defying the Crown of England. They did it because they chose freedom over tyranny, independence over allegiance to an unsympathetic ruler. They wanted to speak, think, and act for themselves without fear. To them all, we owe our freedoms today.

THE DECLARATION OF INDEPENDENCE
(abridged)

IN CONGRESS, July 4, 1776.
The unanimous Declaration of the thirteen united States of America,

When in the Course of human events, it becomes necessary for one people to dissolve the political bands which have connected them with another, and to assume among the powers of the earth, the separate and equal station to which the Laws of Nature and of Nature's God entitle them, a decent respect to the opinions of mankind requires that they should declare the causes which impel them to the separation.

We hold these truths to be self-evident, that all men are created equal, that they are endowed by their Creator with certain unalienable Rights, that among these are Life, Liberty and the pursuit of Happiness.—That to secure these rights, Governments are instituted among Men, deriving their just powers from the consent of the governed,—That whenever any Form of Government becomes destructive of these ends, it is the Right of the People to alter or to abolish it, and to institute new Government, laying its foundation on such principles and organizing its powers in such form, as to them shall seem most likely to effect their Safety and Happiness. Prudence, indeed, will dictate that Governments long established should not be changed for light and transient causes; and accordingly all experience hath shewn, that mankind are more disposed to suffer, while evils are sufferable, than to right themselves by abolishing the forms to which they are accustomed. But when a long train of abuses and usurpations, pursuing invariably the same Object evinces a design to reduce them under absolute Despotism, it is their right, it is their duty, to throw off such Government, and to provide new Guards for their future security.

The signers listed their grievances against the Crown, among them King George's refusal to grant even the simplest requests for self-government and his obstruction of justice. The document ends with these stirring words:

We, therefore, the Representatives of the united States of America, in General Congress, Assembled, appealing to the Supreme Judge of the world for the rectitude of our intentions, do, in the Name, and by Authority of the good People of these Colonies, solemnly publish and declare, That these United Colonies are, and of Right ought to be Free and Independent States; that they are Absolved from all Allegiance to the British Crown, and that all political connection between them and the State of Great Britain, is and ought to be totally dissolved; and that as Free and Independent States, they have full Power to levy War, conclude Peace, contract Alliances, establish Commerce, and to do all other Acts and Things which Independent States may of right do. And for the support of this Declaration, with a firm reliance on the protection of divine Providence, we mutually pledge to each other our Lives, our Fortunes and our sacred Honor.

The United States Constitution
and the Bill of Rights

"We the People of the United States, in Order to form a more perfect Union, establish Justice, insure domestic Tranquility, provide for the common defence, promote the general Welfare, and secure the Blessings of Liberty to ourselves and our Posterity, do ordain and establish this Constitution for the United States of America."

With this preamble, the Articles of Confederation were finalized into a constitution that outlined the system of representative, democratic government that we enjoy today. The strength of our Constitution is its definition of our vibrant, enduring system of checks and balances, established to equalize the power of the three branches of government—the legislative, the executive, and the judicial.

A total of twenty-seven Amendments have been made to the United States Constitution; all protect our essential freedoms. We reprint here the first ten,* which we now refer to as the Bill of

*Other notable amendments include the 13th, which abolished slavery; the 16th, which established an income tax; the 18th, which sought prohibition against alcohol but which was subsequently repealed by the 21st Amendment; the 19th, which gave women the right to vote; the 22nd, which limited presidents to serving two terms, and the 26th, which gave citizens the right to vote at age 18.

Rights, ratified by the original thirteen states on December 15, 1791.

AMENDMENT I   Congress shall make no law respecting an establishment of religion, or prohibiting the free exercise thereof; or abridging the freedom of speech, or of the press; or the right of the people peaceably to assemble, and to petition the Government for a redress of grievances.

AMENDMENT II   A well regulated Militia, being necessary to the security of a free State, the right of the people to keep and bear Arms, shall not be infringed.

AMENDMENT III   No Soldier shall, in time of peace be quartered in any house, without the consent of the Owner, nor in time of war, but in a manner to be prescribed by law.

AMENDMENT IV   The right of the people to be secure in their persons, houses, papers, and effects, against unreasonable searches and seizures, shall not be violated, and no Warrants shall issue, but upon probable cause, supported by Oath or affirmation, and particularly describing the place to be searched, and the persons or things to be seized.

AMENDMENT V   No person shall be held to answer for a capital, or otherwise infamous crime, unless on a presentment or indictment of a Grand Jury, except in cases arising in the land or naval forces, or in the Militia, when in actual service in time of War or public danger; nor shall any person be subject for the same offence to be twice put in jeopardy of life or limb; nor shall be compelled in any criminal case to be a witness against himself, nor be deprived of life, liberty, or property, without due process of law; nor shall private property be taken for public use, without just compensation.

AMENDMENT VI   In all criminal prosecutions, the accused shall enjoy the right to a speedy and public trial, by an impartial jury of the State and district wherein the crime shall have been committed, which district shall have been previously ascertained by law, and to be informed of the nature and cause of the accusation; to be confronted with the witnesses against him; to have compulsory process for obtaining witnesses in his favor, and to have the Assistance of Counsel for his defence.

AMENDMENT VII   In suits at common law, where the value in controversy shall exceed twenty dollars, the right of trial by jury shall be preserved, and no fact tried by a jury, shall be otherwise reexamined in any Court of the United States, than according to the rules of the common law.

AMENDMENT VIII   Excessive bail shall not be required, nor excessive fines imposed, nor cruel and unusual punishments inflicted.

AMENDMENT IX   The enumeration in the Constitution, of certain rights, shall not be construed to deny or disparage others retained by the people.

AMENDMENT X   The powers not delegated to the United States by the Constitution, nor prohibited by it to the States, are reserved to the States respectively, or to the people.

The Gettysburg Address

On November 19, 1863, President Abraham Lincoln traveled by train from Washington, D.C., to the fields of Gettysburg in central Pennsylvania to dedicate a national cemetery for the fallen soldiers of the Civil War. Though more decisive battles had been waged at Vicksburg, Pea Ridge, and Appomattox, it was Gettysburg that became a symbol of the suffering and pain inflicted during the war between Americans. Lincoln's address gives voice to the inexpressible, purpose to the inexplicable. His call for a renewed dedication to freedom for all as a United States of America still rings true for us today, well over a century later.

Five copies of Lincoln's handwritten address are known to have survived. His two personal secretaries, John Nicolay and John Hay, each had one, both of which are now in the Library of Congress. Each extant version varies slightly in editorial detail. Together they offer an intriguing glimpse into Lincoln's approach to writing and his choices of words and phrasing.

The following is believed to be the final version of the address

President Lincoln gave to an audience standing amid the graves of soldiers.

Four score and seven years ago our fathers brought forth upon this continent, a new nation, conceived in liberty, and dedicated to the proposition that "all men are created equal."

Now we are engaged in a great civil war, testing whether that nation, or any nation so conceived, and so dedicated, can long endure. We are met on a great battlefield of that war. We come to dedicate a portion of it, as a final resting place for those who died here, that the nation might live. This we may, in all propriety, do. But, in a larger sense, we can not dedicate—we can not consecrate—we can not hallow, this ground— The brave men, living and dead, who struggled here, have hallowed it, far above our poor power to add or detract. The world will little note, nor long remember what we say here; while it can never forget what they did here.

It is rather for us, the living, we here be dedicated to the great task remaining before us—that, from these honored dead we take increased devotion to that cause for which they here, gave the last full measure of devotion—that we here highly resolve these dead shall not have died in vain; that the nation shall have a new birth of freedom, and that government of the people by the people for the people, shall not perish from the earth.

We Are Fifty States United

E PLURIBUS UNUM: ONE OUT OF MANY

What began as a group of thirteen colonies has grown into a united country of fifty states. All are blessed with exceptional natural beauty, large cities and rural communities, and the citizens of each are guaranteed the freedoms of life, liberty, and the pursuit of happiness our Founding Fathers proposed. Here is a sampling of what makes every state unique, accompanied by the names of some accomplished Americans native to each.*

1. **Delaware**, December 7, 1787. The first to ratify the U.S. Constitution, Delaware is now home to one of the world's finest gardens at the Winterthur Museum, Garden and Library. This small state boasts beautiful family beaches and resorts. *We're proud of these Delawareans:* inventor-surgeon Henry Heimlich, Thomas Garrett (who helped thousands of fugitive slaves move along the Underground Railroad), Valerie Bertinelli, artist Howard Pyle, E. I. Du Pont, Estelle Taylor . . .

*The states are listed in order of admittance to the union, followed by the date.

2. **Pennsylvania**, December 12, 1787. This state is a treasure trove of Revolutionary War sites and home to Gettysburg, where President Abraham Lincoln made his famous address. Independence Hall and the Liberty Bell are in Philadelphia, once the capital of the country. Chocolate lovers will find their dreams coming true in Hershey. *We're proud of these Pennsylvanians:* W. C. Fields, Bill Cosby, General George C. Marshall, Andy Warhol, Arnold Palmer, B. F. Skinner, Reggie Jackson, Rachel Carson, Louisa May Alcott, Daniel Boone, Stephen Foster, Gene Kelly, Margaret Mead, Gertrude Stein, Andrew Wyeth . . .

3. **New Jersey**, December 18, 1787. The Garden State, where the Appalachian Mountains are breathtaking, the farmland rich, and the manufacturing profitable. Beautiful beaches and grand homes grace its ocean shore. *We're proud of these New Jerseyans:* U.S. Presidents Grover Cleveland and Richard M. Nixon, Charles Addams, Paul Robeson, Frank Sinatra, astronaut Edwin "Buzz" Aldrin, dancer Ruth St. Denis, Bud Abbott *and* Lou Costello, Norman Mailer, Bruce Springsteen, William Carlos Williams, Count Basie, Allen Ginsberg, Rick Nelson . . .

4. **Georgia**, January 2, 1788. Home to the world's largest infantry training center, Fort Benning; the Atlanta Braves; and to Coca-Cola, not to mention peanuts, pecans, peaches, and to Wesleyan College in Macon, the first college in the world chartered to grant degrees to women. *We're proud of these Georgians:* U.S. President Jimmy Carter, Jessye Norman, Ray Charles, Ty Cobb, Alice Walker, James Dickey, Little Richard, Martin Luther King Jr., Jackie Robinson, Joanne Woodward, Jasper Johns . . .

5. Connecticut, January 9, 1788. The first steel mill in the United States was built here (in 1728), as was the first nuclear-powered submarine, the U.S.S. *Nautilus* (1954), Connecticut is home to the longest continually published newspaper in the country, *The Hartford Courant. We're proud of these Nutmeggers:* P. T. Barnum, Charles Ives, Frederick Law Olmsted, Dr. Benjamin Spock, Katharine Hepburn, Harriet Beecher Stowe, Dorothy Hamill . . .

6. Massachusetts, February 6, 1788. Dozens of our best colleges can be found here, as can Boston beans, the Boston Red Sox, the Boston Pops, and Boston. *We're proud of these Bay Staters:* U.S. presidents John Adams, John Quincy Adams, John F. Kennedy, and the elder George Bush, nurseryman John Chapman, (a.k.a. Johnny Appleseed), Paul Revere, Cecil B. DeMille, Benjamin Franklin, Eli Whitney, Elias Howe, Leonard Bernstein, Emily Dickinson, Edgar Allan Poe, Dr. Seuss (Theodore Geisel), Barbara Walters . . .

7. Maryland, April 28, 1788. Chesapeake Bay crabs and crab cakes. The Orioles and the Ravens. One of our finest colleges and medical institutions: Johns Hopkins. *We're proud of these Marylanders:* Eubie Blake, Billie Holiday, Babe Ruth, Upton Sinclair, H. L. Mencken, Leon Uris, Frederick Douglass, Samuel Chase, Thurgood Marshall, Roger B. Taney, Spiro T. Agnew, Frank Zappa, Frank Perdue . . .

8. South Carolina, May 23, 1788. Off its coast, on Wadmalaw Island, is the only tea-growing plantation in the country. The state also boasts the vacation and business paradise Hilton Head. *We're proud of these South Carolinians:* Bernard Baruch, Joe Frazier,

Althea Gibson, Dizzy Gillespie, journalist Charlayne Hunter-Gault, James Brown, Chubby Checker, Strom Thurmond, Jesse Jackson, Eartha Kitt, General William Westmoreland . . .

9. **New Hampshire**, June 21, 1788. Christian Science began here, Horace Greeley went west from here, Daniel Webster grappled with devilish politics. Skiing in winter, camping in summer. Dartmouth. *We're proud of these New Hampshirites:* U.S. President Franklin Pierce, Mary Baker Eddy, Judy Blum, John Irving, astronaut Alan Shepard, jurist Harlan F. Stone . . .

10. **Virginia**, June 25, 1788. More U.S. presidents were born here than in any other state: Thomas Jefferson, William H. Harrison, James Madison, James Monroe, Zachary Taylor, John Tyler, George Washington, and Woodrow Wilson. Visiting Virginia is a trip through American history: Revolutionary War battlegrounds, Appomattox and other Civil War sites; Jefferson's Monticello, eighteenth-century Williamsburg; the modern naval shipyards at Roanoke. And beautiful mountains and mountain music, too. *We're also proud of these Virginians:* Arthur Ashe, Russell Baker, Admiral Richard E. Byrd, Willa Cather, Roy Clark, Shirley MacLaine and Warren Beatty, Booker T. Washington, Ella Fitzgerald . . .

11. **New York**, July 26, 1788. Home to the Statue of Liberty, Ellis Island, and the other wonders of New York City, American theater and fine arts, the United Nations. The Adirondacks. Apple orchards and dairy farms. The Yankees and the Mets, the Knicks, the Giants, the Jets, and the Islanders. A citizenry that comes from everywhere originally. *We're proud of these New Yorkers:* Lou

Gehrig, Eleanor Roosevelt, Margaret Sanger, George Westinghouse Jr., George Eastman, Louis Comfort Tiffany, John D. Rockefeller, Walt Whitman, Herman Melville, Ogden Nash, Billy Joel, Lucille Ball, Michael Jordan, Maria Callas, Ethel Merman, Sammy Davis Jr., John Jay, Learned Hand, Charles Evans Hughes, Vince Lombardi, Kareem Abdul-Jabbar, U.S. Presidents Theodore Roosevelt, Franklin D. Roosevelt, Millard Fillmore, and Martin Van Buren, and the firefighters, policemen, and city officials of the great city of New York . . .

12. **North Carolina**, November 21, 1789. The Biltmore Estate, the Blue Ridge Mountains and the rest of the Appalachians, scenic Winston-Salem, the Moravians; the bustling Raleigh-Durham area, Duke University and the Blue Devils, Chapel Hill, Kitty Hawk, the small beach where the Wright Brothers flew that famous plane. *We're proud of these North Carolinians:* Reverend Billy Graham, industrialist James B. Duke, Elizabeth Hanford Dole, David Brinkley, Floyd Patterson, Soupy Sales, Earl Scruggs, O. Henry, Howard Cosell, Ava Gardner, Roberta Flack . . .

13. **Rhode Island**, May 29, 1790. The Ocean State and the smallest of them all. Site of beautiful beaches, the Gilded Age "cottages" of Newport, and the oldest synagogue in America. *We're proud of these Rhode Islanders:* George M. Cohan, lighthouse keeper Ida Lewis, Spalding Gray, portraitist Gilbert Stuart, poet Galway Kinnell, Nelson Eddy . . .

14. **Vermont**, March 4, 1791. Maple syrup, arts-and-crafters, and the Green Mountains; skiing up a storm. The gold dome of the capital building. *We're proud of these Vermonters:* U.S. Presidents

Calvin Coolidge and Chester Alan Arthur, inventors John Deere and Elisha Otis, Brigham Young, Admiral George Dewey, Rudy Vallee, John Dewey . . .

15. **Kentucky**, June 1, 1792. The grass in some areas really does look blue green, the horses race every May in the Derby, and something inspirational must be in the water to produce such fine writers, artists, craftspeople, and one great monk, Thomas Merton. *We're also proud of these Kentuckians:* Bobbie Ann Mason, Hunter S. Thompson, Loretta Lynn, Don and Phil Everly, Rosemary Clooney, President Abraham Lincoln . . .

16. **Tennessee**, June 1, 1796. Storytelling and folklore abound. And Tennessee has Nashville and the Grand Ole Opry as well as Memphis and Beale Street, Graceland, and the National Civil Rights Museum. *We're proud of these Tennesseans:* Red Grooms, James Agee, Nikki Giovanni, Eddy Arnold, Aretha Franklin, Bill Monroe, Chet Atkins, Davy Crockett, Dolly Parton, Dinah Shore, Tina Turner, Minnie Pearl . . .

17. **Ohio**, March 1, 1803. Farming, rubber tires, and some of the best symphonies and museums you'll find anywhere. Ohio State and the Ohio River. Birthplace of eight U.S. presidents: James Garfield, William Howard Taft, William Harding, William McKinley, Rutherford Hayes, Benjamin Harrison, and Ulysses Grant. *We're also proud of these Ohioans:* Neil Armstrong, architect Maya Lin, Jack Nicklaus, James Thurber, Wilbur and Orville Wright, Annie Oakley, Chrissie Hynde, Thomas Edison, Chief Tecumseh . . .

18. **Louisiana**, April 30, 1812. Mardi Gras. Preservation Hall and all that jazz. The Bayou country, Tulane and Baylor. Steaming hot beignets and chicory coffee. *We're proud of these Louisianans:* Wynton and Branford Marsalis, Jerry Lee Lewis, Mahalia Jackson, Jelly Roll Morton, Fats Domino, Van Cliburn, Louis Armstrong, Pete Fountain, Al Hirt, Paul Prudhomme, Truman Capote, Lillian Hellman, Anne Rice, Geoffrey Beene, Bryant Gumbel, Henry Connick Jr. . . .

19. **Indiana**, December 11, 1816. Every Memorial Day since 1911, the Indianapolis Motor Speedway has hosted the Indianapolis 500. Over 100 species of trees are native to the state, and the richest limestone deposits anywhere have supplied building material for fourteen state capitols, the Pentagon, Rockefeller Center, and the Empire State Building. The first-ever professional baseball game took place in Fort Wayne on May 4, 1871. *We're proud of these Indianans:* Ernie Pyle, Cole Porter, Larry Bird, Bill Blass, James Whitcomb Riley, Red Skelton, David Letterman, James Dean, Michael Jackson, Janet Jackson, John Mellencamp . . .

20. **Mississippi**, December 10, 1817. A state that breeds great writers, steamboat gamblers, and romance. Riverboat gamblers now have legitimate casinos to play in beside the mighty Mississippi River that runs through this state, the catfish capital of the world. The Gulf Islands National Seashore, Vicksburg National Military Park, and stately plantations draw thousands of visitors each year. *We're proud of these Mississippians:* Shelby Foote, Oprah Winfrey, Jimmy Buffett, William Faulkner, Beth Henley, Red Barber,

Charles and Medgar Evers, Tammy Wynette, Bo Diddley, B. B. King, Tennessee Williams, Elvis Presley . . .

21. Illinois, December 3, 1818. Abraham Lincoln grew up here, and this state was the first to ratify the Thirteenth Amendment, abolishing slavery in 1865. Illinois is home to the world's first skyscraper, built in 1885, and the tallest building on the continent, the Sears Tower, both in Chicago, a city where you can find a team to cheer for, no matter what sport you love most: the Bears, the Blackhawks, the Bulls, the Cubs, the White Sox, and the Fire. A premier marketplace. The Museum of Science and Industry and at least twenty more museums in Chicago alone. *We're proud of these Illinoisans:* President Ronald Reagan, Walt Disney, Raymond Chandler, Ray Bradbury, Miles Davis, Curtis Mayfield, Jane Addams (founder of Hull House), Dorothy Hamill, Quincy Jones, Carl Sandburg, Sam Shepard, David Mamet, New York Senator Hillary Rodham Clinton . . .

22. Alabama, December 14, 1819. The first trolley system was introduced in Montgomery in 1886. Iron and steel workers from Alabama built rockets that sent the first humans to the moon. Alabama's Miss America, Heather Whitestone (1995), was the first selected with a disability (deafness). *We're also proud of these Alabamans:* Chief Tascaluza (Choctaw), Nat "King" Cole, Emmylou Harris, Tallulah Bankhead, Willie Mays, Lionel Richie, Hank Aaron, Joe Louis, Coretta Scott King, Helen Keller, Rosa Parks, Jesse Owens . . .

23. **Maine**, March 15, 1820. One of the most healthful places to live, this state boasts unusual beauty (the 92-mile Allagash National Wilderness Waterway), one of the most visited national parks (Acadia), and provides about half the lobsters and 99 percent of all the blueberries grown in America. Its rugged and rocky shore has inspired writers and painters for generations. *We're proud of these Mainers:* Dorothea Dix, Henry Wadsworth Longfellow, Senator Margaret Chase Smith, John Ford, Edna St. Vincent Millay, Linda Lavin, George Putnam, F. Lee Bailey, Stephen King . . .

24. **Missouri**, August 10, 1821. You can dance the "Missouri Waltz" in the rolling hills of the thoroughly Midwestern "Show Me State." Harry S. Truman owned a haberdashery store in Independence before becoming FDR's vice president. When FDR died, the country learned that HST meant it when he said, "The buck stops here." There's Kansas City barbecue, the music at the Branson theaters, and the quiet serenity of the Jamesport Amish. And there's the drama of the largest manmade monument in the country: St. Louis's Gateway Arch. *We're also proud of these Missourians:* Virgil Thomson, J. C. Penney, George Washington Carver, astronomer Edwin Hubble, General Omar N. Bradley, Mark Twain, T. S. Eliot, Sara Teasdale, Marianne Moore, Langston Hughes, Yogi Berra, Casey Stengel, Al Hirschfield, Walter Cronkite . . .

25. **Arkansas**, June 15, 1836. The Ozark Mountains cover more than one million acres and the state has 600,000 acres of lakes and 9,700 miles of streams and rivers, making it a fisherman's utopia. Its Quapaw Quarter showcases Victorian and antebellum homes; the state is the world's center for archery bow production and

produces the world's largest selection of handmade dulcimers. *We're proud of these Arkansans:* Sam Walton, founder of Wal-Mart, General Douglas MacArthur; President Bill Clinton, Johnny Cash, Maya Angelou, Helen Gurley Brown, John Grisham, Alan Ladd Sr., architect Edward Durell Stone . . .

26. **Michigan**, January 26, 1837. It has the auto industry. It has Motown. And it has world-class restaurants and world-renowned universities. This Great Lakes state is a fisherman's paradise, but don't forget the tulips (in Holland, natch) and all the breakfast cereal you can imagine in Battle Creek, home of health guru W. K. Kellogg. *We're proud of these Michiganders:* Stevie Wonder, Lily Tomlin, Diana Ross, Bob Seger, Della Reese, Madonna, Charles A. Lindbergh, Earvin "Magic" Johnson, astronaut Roger Chaffee, Ralph J. Bunche, Henry Ford, Terry McMillan, Robin Williams . . .

27. **Florida**, March 3, 1845. Home of spring training for major league baseball, the one-of-a-kind Florida Museum of Hispanic and Latin American Art, South Beach, Coral Gables, Atlantic shrimp, the Everglades, Disney World, the Morikami Museum and Japanese Gardens, sunny retirement communities, great beaches, golf courses, Cape Kennedy, the Florida Keys. *We're proud of these Floridians:* Jim Morrison, Pat Boone, Julian "Cannonball" Adderley, Ben Vereen, Tom Petty, Dwight Gooden, General Joseph W. Stilwell, Zora Neale Hurston, astronaut Norman E. Thargard . . .

28. **Texas**, December 29, 1845. The huge homeland of cattle ranches, oil wells, the Alamo, and barbecue. Fishing and boating

in the Gulf of Mexico. Texas A&M and the University of Texas. "The Yellow Rose of Texas." Houston, Dallas, the Lyndon B. Johnson Space Center, and Austin. *We're proud of these Texans:* Molly Ivins, Howard Hughes, Carol Burnett, Liz Smith, cosmetics queen Mary Kay Ash, Alvin Ailey, Babe Didrikson Zaharias, Janis Joplin, Ben Hogan, A. J. Foyt, Buddy Holly, Don Henley, and U.S. Presidents George W. Bush, Lyndon B. Johnson, and Dwight David Eisenhower . . .

29. **Iowa**, December 28, 1846. First in pork, first in corn, and first in soybean production, Iowa also raises lots of bright kids: For the last twenty years, their youth has led the nation in SAT and ACT scores. The covered-bridge capital of the country, it was the film location for *The Bridges of Madison County*, and its scenic cornfields were the backdrop for *Field of Dreams*. The Iowa Writers' Workshop and the Effigy Mounds National Monument. Claims to have the crookedest street in the world: Snake Alley, in the southeast. *We're proud of these Iowans:* Grant Wood, George Gallup, Frederick L. Maytag, Ann Landers and Abigail Van Buren, John Wayne, Glenn Miller, Johnny Carson . . .

30. **Wisconsin**, May 29, 1848. Beer and dairy products are this state's claim to fame, but it's also the paper-making capital of the country. You can fish for Chinook salmon and Northern Pike and spy eagles in their natural habitats in Sauk City or Cassville, visit the Great Lakes or parts of the Mississippi via canoe or steamboat, have fun skiing or snowshoeing, or join the mania for golfing at one of hundreds of great courses. *We're proud of these Wisconsinites:* Jeanne Dixon, Harry Houdini, Liberace, Georgia O'Keeffe, Thornton Wilder, Orson Welles . . .

31. **California**, September 9, 1850. This state has the largest economy of any state. Los Angeles is the heart of the American entertainment industry. The Golden Gate Bridge, the Giants, the Padres, the Angels, and the A's, Sequoia National Park, home to the largest living tree (102 feet in circumference), Mount Whitney, Disneyland, Highway 101, the Hollywood Bowl, Malibu. Death Valley is the hottest, driest place in the country. *We're proud of these Californians:* Everybody is famous in California, at least for a few minutes, but Marilyn Monroe, Jerry Garcia, all the original Beach Boys, Natalie Cole, Cher, Debbie Reynolds, Julia Child, Robert Frost, Jack London, astronaut Sally Ride, Joe DiMaggio, and Sally Fields actually were born in California. Everyone else is from out of town . . .

32. **Minnesota**, May 11, 1858. Superior National Forest, the Mayo Clinic, dynamic twin cities of Minneapolis/St. Paul. Great lakes, great universities, and sweet towns to raise kids the worry-free way. The current governor is a former pro wrestler. *We're proud of these Minnesotans:* Bob Dylan, Roger Maris, Judy Garland, Garrison Keillor, the Andrews Sisters, Walter Mondale, F. Scott Fitzgerald, Prince, Harrison Salisbury, Charles M. Schulz . . .

33. **Oregon**, February 14, 1859. The wine, berry, and fruit capital of the Pacific Northwest. Mount Hood, Crater Lake, and the Bonneville Dam. Fantastic rose, Japanese, and Chinese gardens. *We're proud of these Oregonians:* Raymond Carver, Dave Kingman, John Reede, James Beard, Linus Pauling, Matt Groening . . .

34. **Kansas**, January 29, 1861. Dorothy came back, and no wonder! Clean air, golden wheat fields, endless sky, and the easiest-to-

navigate airport in the country. *We're proud of these Kansans:* Amelia Earhart, Zasu Pitts, Buster Keaton, William Inge, Gordon Parks, Senator Robert Dole, Damon Runyon, Emmett Kelly . . .

35. **West Virginia**, June 20, 1863. This beautiful mountain state has valuable lumber, coal, and minerals, but its real gems are its recreational pleasures: numerous historical Civil War sites and railways, Seneca Caverns, thousands of acres of wildlife preserves and state forests. *We're proud of these West Virginians:* Don Knotts, George Brett, Kathy Mattea, Pearl S. Buck, Chuck Yeager, Mary-Lou Retton . . .

36. **Nevada**, October 31, 1864. Las Vegas is now a family entertainment destination, but all that gambling still means no one has to pay state taxes. There is major beauty in the Nevada Desert and powerful Hoover Dam is on view, too. *We're proud of these Nevadans:* Andre Agassi, Paiute peacemaker Sarah Hopkins Winnemucca, Pat Nixon, Luke Pease, Walter Van Tilburg Clark . . .

37. **Nebraska**, March 1, 1867. The still beauty of the prairies and wheatfields. The Cornhusker State is headquarters for the U.S. Strategic Command and boasts the Western Hemisphere's largest acreage of sandhill grasslands, plus amazing fossil beds, the great Platte River, and magnificent Scotts Bluff. *We're proud of these Nebraskans:* Warren Buffett, U.S. president Gerald Ford, Fred Astaire, Dick Cavett, Marlon Brando, Malcolm X . . .

38. **Colorado**, August 1, 1876. Hosted the world's first rodeo on July 4, 1869, in Deer Trail; fantastic natural wonders from the highest sand dune in the country (Great Sand Dunes National Monu-

ment) to the Colorado Rockies, Mesa Verde, a four-story city carved into the cliffs by Pueblo Indians, dates to 1300 A.D. The Continental Divide, the Colorado School of Mines, awesome skiing. *We're proud of these Coloradans:* Mattel founder Ruth Handler, creator of the Barbie doll; Jack Dempsey, astronaut M. Scott Carpenter, Ute Indian Chief Ouray . . .

39 and 40. North Dakota and South Dakota, both admitted on November 2, 1889. The endless bright blue sky watched over Lewis and Clark's expedition as it traveled through these states, land of prairies, the Badlands and the Black Hills, that wild combination of valleys, grasslands, and austere mountains. South Dakota is the home of Mount Rushmore. *We're proud of these South Dakotans:* Tom Brokaw, Russell Means, Sioux chiefs Sitting Bull and Red Cloud, and Hubert H. Humphrey. *We're also proud of these North Dakotans:* General David C. Jones, Eric Sevareid, James Rosenquist, Warren Christopher, Lawrence Welk, Peggy Lee, Angie Dickinson, Larry Woiwode, Louis L'Amour, William H. Gass . . .

41. Montana, November 8, 1889. Montana, part of the Big Sky Country, is still the fierce land of the settler, the farmer, the rancher, and the individualist that inspired Richard Hugo, Norman McLean, Wallace Earle Stegner, and Thomas McGuane to write about its white cliffs, wildlife refuges, serene fishing, the Glacier and Yellowstone national park areas and the people of character, independence, and fierce loyalty of their neighbors. *We're also proud of these Montanans:* Evel Knievel, Gary Cooper, David Lynch, A. B. Guthrie . . .

42. **Washington**, November 11, 1889. The wine and the food: coffee and apples and Pacific salmon. The burgeoning metropolis of Seattle and the Space Needle. The most wonderful combination of land and water activities available anywhere. *We're proud of these Washingtonians:* astronaut Francis Scobee, Robert Motherwell, Merce Cunningham, Robert Joffrey, Carol Channing, Gypsy Rose Lee, Judy Collins, Jimi Hendrix, Bing Crosby, Chuck Jones . . .

43. **Idaho**, July 3, 1890. Idaho is no small potatoes, it's the number-one producer of trout, Austrian winter peas, and lentils, too. Filmmakers are taking notice of its Sawtooth Mountains, fly fishing streams and lakes, and the unique four-state view from Heaven's Gate Lookout, in the Seven Devils' Peaks range. The home of the Appaloosa horse, and the densest population in the nation of nesting eagles, hawks, and falcons reside in the Birds of Prey National Conservation Area. Idaho also has the largest man-made geyser in the world in Soda Springs. *We're proud of these Idahoans:* Gutzon Borglum, sculptor of Mount Rushmore, Lana Turner, Picabo Street, Ezra Pound . . .

44. **Wyoming**, July 10, 1890. Cowboys still ride into town—but note that women have equal footing here. While it was still a territory, in 1869, Wyoming granted women the right to vote, the first government in the world to do so. Here are the natural wonders of Yellowstone National Park, the hot springs, and Old Faithful, the Grand Tetons, and gigantic sheep pastures (Wyoming is the country's second largest wool producer). *We're proud of these Wyomingsites:* Shoshone Chief Washakei; Curt Gowdy, Jackson Pollock . . .

45. Utah, January 4, 1896. From Great Salt Lake to the magnificent Bryce Canyon, this is the state for the outdoor recreation enthusiast. Its burnt-red earth and magnificent sunsets are unforgettable. Archaeological digs in the Utah desert have unearthed human remains dating back at least 10,000 years. Home to Brigham Young University and the site of the 2002 Winter Olympics. *We're proud of these Utahans:* Reed Smoot (the first Mormon to be elected to the U.S. Senate), J. Willard Marriott, Roseanne, Merlin Olsen, Philo T. Farnsworth (inventor of television), and all of the Osmonds (except Jimmy) . . .

46. Oklahoma, November 16, 1907. Rodeos and oil wells, great universities and tiny hamlets, all are part of Oklahoma, the Sooner State. Sophisticated Tulsa—and yes, crossword buffs, Ada and Enid can really be found here. *We're proud of these Oklahomans:* Maria Tallchief, Jeane Kirkpatrick, James Garner, Woody Guthrie, Reba McEntire, Ralph Ellison, Tony Hillerman, Brad Pitt, Oral Roberts, Jim Thorpe, Mickey Mantle, Johnny Bench, Garth Brooks, Will Rogers, poet John Berryman, Ralph Ellison, Chester Gould . . .

47. New Mexico, January 6, 1912. Taos has its pueblos, our creative Native Americans' idea for "apartment living," and Santa Fe has its Opera, and Governor's Square, where you can get a sopapilla, buy silver and turquoise jewelry and paintings, sculpture, and crafts. Powwows and winter skiing, horse races and outdoor living, Carlsbad Caverns and wide open spaces—all set under the dazzling sky over this Land of Enchantment. *We're proud of these New Mexicans:* Bill Mauldin, Apache leader Mangus Coloradas, physicist Edward Condon, astronaut Sid Gutierrez, John Denver, William Hanna, Demi Moore . . .

48. **Arizona**, February 14, 1912. Sedona, the mighty Grand Canyon, the Petrified Forest, and the Painted Desert are only part of the everyday wonder of this state. Astronomers from around the world trek to Flagstaff for its magnificent telescope and the possibility of discovering new planets or stars. The only state to observe Mountain Standard Time year round—except on the Navajo Nation. Late winter and early spring, it's "play ball" time as baseball teams practice for the season ahead. *We're proud of these Arizonans:* Cochise, Geronimo, Cesar Chavez, Linda Ronstadt, Stevie Nicks, Lynda Carter, Charles Mingus, WWI fighter ace Frank Luke Jr. . . .

49. **Alaska**, January 3, 1959. Seventeen of the twenty highest peaks in the U.S. are here, including Mount McKinley, the highest point in the U.S. It is home to the Tongass National Forest, our largest, and the peculiarities of long days of darkness in winter and long days of sun in summer, the better to enjoy fishing for salmon, crab, halibut, and herring or training the dogs to mush for the Iditarod. Among its other natural resources are 25 percent of the nation's oil, great timber forests, and plenty of gold. *We're proud of these Alaskans:* prospector Joe Juneau (he discovered gold), Carl Ben Eielson (pioneer pilot), cartoonist Virgil F. Partch . . .

50. **Hawaii**, August 21, 1959. Formerly a foreign country ruled by royalty, it is our newest state and the only one that grows coffee, pineapples, and macadamia nuts. About 2,390 miles from the

mainland, the islands that form Hawaii are the projecting tops of the biggest mountain range in the world and include Kilauea Iki, the world's youngest and most active volcano. Hawaii has its own time zone (Hawaiian Standard Time) with no daylight savings time and fabulously benign weather. *We're proud of these Hawaiians:* astronaut Ellison Onizuka, Olympic swimmer Duke Paoa Kahanamoku, Tia Carrere, Bette Midler, Steve Case . . .

The Pledge of Allegiance

Francis Bellamy (1855–1931), a Baptist minister and Christian Socialist, wrote the original Pledge in August 1892, echoing the ideas of his first cousin, the writer Edward Bellamy. The two believed in an American socialist utopia in which the government would run a peacetime economy and the people would live with political, social, and economic equality for all. As first published in the September 8, 1892, issue of *The Youth's Companion* (the *Reader's Digest* of its time), the pledge originally read: "I pledge allegiance to my flag and (to*) the Republic for which it stands, one nation, indivisible, with liberty and justice for all."

In 1923 and 1924 the American Legion and the Daughters of the American Revolution lobbied to change the words from "my flag" to "the flag of the United States of America)." In 1954, the Knights of Columbus campaigned to urge Congress (which did not officially recognize the pledge until 1942) to add the words "under God." The Pledge is now considered both a patriotic oath and a public prayer.

* The "to" was added in October 1892.

The true reason for allegiance to the Flag is the "republic for which it stands." . . . And what does that vast thing, the Republic mean? It is the concise political word for the Nation—the One Nation—which the Civil War was fought to prove. To make that One Nation idea clear, we must specify that it is indivisible . . .

—Francis Bellamy

OUR GOVERNMENT

Does the government fear us? Or do we fear the government? When the people fear the government, tyranny has found victory. The federal government is our servant, not our master!

—Thomas Jefferson

"The Four Freedoms"

PRESIDENT FRANKLIN D. ROOSEVELT

From an address to the Congress of the United States on January 6, 1941—almost a year before the attack on Pearl Harbor, December 7, the same year.

In the future days, which we seek to make secure, we look forward to a world founded upon four essential human freedoms.

The first is freedom of speech and expression—everywhere in the world.

The second is freedom of every person to worship God in his own way—everywhere in the world.

The third is freedom from want—which, translated into world terms, means economic understandings which will secure to every nation a healthy peacetime life for its inhabitants—everywhere in the world.

The fourth is freedom from fear—which, translated into world terms, means a worldwide reduction of armaments to such a point and in such a thorough fashion that no nation will be in a position to commit an act of physical aggression against any neighbor—anywhere in the world.

That is no vision of a distant millennium. It is a definite basis for a kind of world attainable in our own time and generation. That kind of world is the very antithesis of the so-called new order of tyranny which the dictators seek to create with the crash of a bomb.

To that new order we oppose the greater conception—the moral order. A good society is able to face schemes of world domination and foreign revolutions alike without fear. . . . Freedom means the supremacy of human rights everywhere. Our support goes to those who struggle to gain those rights or keep them. Our strength is our unity of purpose.

To that high concept there can be no end save victory.

U.S. Presidents and Vice Presidents

For more than two centuries our country has been governed by a democratic process that includes free elections. Political parties have changed, the process has evolved, and the safeguards for the transition of power have been tested and found to work in times of death, resignation, or other difficult crises.

We have had forty-one presidents. Fourteen of them had previously served as vice president.* Here is a listing of the leaders who have governed this proud union:

Years Served	*President*	*Vice President*
1789–1797	George Washington	John Adams
1797–1801	John Adams	Thomas Jefferson
1801–1809	Thomas Jefferson	Aaron Burr
		George Clinton

*Several presidents had more than one vice president because of resignation, death, or, in the case of Franklin D. Roosevelt, because he was elected to three terms rather than the now-mandated two. The Adamses and the Bushes are the only families in which both father and son have served. (The Roosevelts were from different branches of the same family.)

Years Served	President	Vice President
1809–1817	James Madison	George Clinton Elbridge Gerry
1817–1825	James Monroe	Daniel D. Tompkins
1825–1829	John Quincy Adams	John C. Calhoun
1829–1837	Andrew Jackson	John C. Calhoun (resigned) Martin Van Buren
1837–1841	Martin Van Buren	Richard M. Johnson (elected by the Senate)
1841	William H. Harrison	John Tyler
1841–1845	John Tyler	none
1845–1849	James K. Polk	George M. Dallas
1849–1850	Zachary Taylor	Millard Fillmore
1850–1853	Millard Fillmore	none
1853–1857	Franklin Pierce	William R. King
1857–1861	James Buchanan	John C. Breckinridge
1861–1865	Abraham Lincoln	Hannibal Hamlin Andrew Johnson
1865–1869	Andrew Johnson	none
1869–1877	Ulysses S. Grant	Schuyler Colfax Henry Wilson
1877–1881	Rutherford B. Hayes	William A. Wheeler
1881	James A. Garfield	Chester A. Arthur
1881–1885	Chester A. Arthur	none
1885–1889	S. Grover Cleveland	Thomas A. Hendricks
1889–1893	Benjamin Harrison	Levi P. Morton
1893–1897	S. Grover Cleveland	Adlai E. Stevenson Sr.
1897–1901	William McKinley	Garret A. Hobart Theodore Roosevelt

Years Served	*President*	*Vice President*
1901–1909	Theodore Roosevelt	Charles W. Fairbanks
1909–1913	William Howard Taft	James S. Sherman
1913–1921	(Thomas) Woodrow Wilson	Thomas R. Marshall
1921–1923	Warren G. Harding	Calvin Coolidge
1923–1929	Calvin Coolidge	Charles G. Dawes
1929–1933	Herbert C. Hoover	Charles Curtis
1933–1945	Franklin Delano Roosevelt	John N. Garner
		Henry A. Wallace
		Harry S. Truman
1945–1953	Harry S. Truman (elected by the Senate)	Alben W. Barkley
1953–1961	Dwight D. Eisenhower	Richard M. Nixon
1961–1963	John F. Kennedy	Lyndon B. Johnson
1963–1969	Lyndon B. Johnson	Hubert H. Humphrey
1969–1974	Richard M. Nixon (resigned)	Spiro T. Agnew (resigned)
		Gerald R. Ford (appointed under the Twenty-fifth amendment)
1974–1977	Gerald R. Ford	Nelson Rockefeller (appointed under the Twenty-fifth Amendment)
1977–1981	James (Jimmy) Carter	Walter F. Mondale
1981–1989	Ronald W. Reagan	George H. Walker Bush
1989–1993	George H. Walker Bush	J. Danforth Quayle
1993–2001	William Jefferson Clinton	Albert Gore
2001–	George W. Bush	Richard (Dick) B. Cheney

Who's Who in the Cabinet

The Cabinet is an unelected council of advisers to the president, and each Cabinet member is responsible for the enforcement of laws and regulations governing the federal agency he or she heads. By law, the Cabinet includes the vice president and executive departments that now number fourteen. With the exception of the U.S. Attorney General and the vice president, the Cabinet members are referred to as secretaries. The Attorney General is, in effect, the prosecutor for the government in various cases.

The Cabinet consists of many departments that have evolved with the country's needs. Its members' advisory role has been explicit since the Constitution was written, and its purposes are officially decreed in Article II, Section 2.

President Bush has a vivid cross-section of Americans in his Cabinet with representatives from Asian, Hispanic, African-American, and other cultures, plus four women:

Attorney General: John Ashcroft
Secretary of Agriculture: Ann M. Veneman
Secretary of Commerce: Donald Evans
Secretary of Defense: Donald H. Rumsfeld
Secretary of Education: Roderick Paige
Secretary of Energy: Spencer Abraham
Secretary of Health and Human Services: Tommy G. Thompson
Secretary for Housing and Urban Development: Mel Martinez
Secretary of Interior: Gale A. Norton
Secretary of Labor: Elaine Chao
Secretary of State: Colin Powell
Secretary of Transportation: Norman Mineta
Secretary of the Treasury: Paul H. O'Neill
Secretary of Veterans' Affairs: Anthony J. Principi

CABINET RANK MEMBERS

The Vice President: Richard (Dick) B. Cheney
President's Chief of Staff: Andrew H. Card Jr.
Environmental Protection Agency: Christie Todd Whitman
Office of Management and Budget Director: Mitchell E. Daniels Jr.
Office of National Drug Control Policy: John P. Walters (nominee at press time)
United States Trade Representative Ambassador: Robert B. Zoellick

Take It to the Supreme Court

It is 10 A.M., the first Monday of October, and a marshal declares, "The Honorable, the chief justice and the associate justices of the Supreme Court of the United States. Oyez! Oyez! Oyez!" Nine black-robed men and women enter the chamber and are seated at the highly polished mahogany bench. There they work to defend our liberties and supervise equal justice under the law. They will hear cases, review petitions, and write decisions from October through June, and in the other months and other days of the week, they will write opinions, decide what other cases to review, study, and consult.

The tradition began on February 1, 1790, in the Merchants Exchange Building in New York City, then the nation's capital. Some justices arrived a day later because of traffic. (Some things have not changed!) For 101 years, the justices "rode circuit" throughout the states where they held court twice a year in each judicial district.

The Court had several different "homes" until 1935, when the Supreme Court Building in Washington, D.C., opened. The building included marble from Alabama, Vermont, and Georgia; American white oak; many magnificent brass and wood details; and huge sculptures depicting the rights and freedoms of the United States. The court building's total cost was *less* than the $9,740,000 allotted by Congress. Both building and the furnishings came in under budget, and the surplus was returned to the Treasury.

Today attorneys arguing cases before the bench experience tradition (black robes were first worn in 1800) and anachronism (white quill pens adorn the attorneys' tables) alongside access to the most sophisticated electronic information retrieval systems and 450,000 volumes of the nation's laws in the court library. The court is open to the public, guests of the justices, and visiting dignitaries. Each group has its own special benches and chairs in either elegant black (guests) or red (the press).

The number of justices has changed several times, but since 1869 the number has been nine: a chief justice and eight associate justices. Each is appointed by the president with approval by Congress, and all terms of office are for life.

The present court is comprised of Chief Justice William H. Rehnquist, the oldest at eighty-one, with Associate Justice Clarence Thomas the youngest, age fifty-three. The other associate justices are Sandra Day O'Connor, Ruth Bader Ginsburg, David H. Souter, Antonin Scalia, John Paul Stevens, Stephen G. Breyer, and Anthony M. Kennedy.

Among the "firsts" to be named to the court are Roger B. Taney, the first Catholic justice; Louis Brandeis, the first Jew;

Thurgood Marshall, the first African American; and Sandra Day O'Connor, the first woman. Chief Justice William O. Douglas served the longest: 36 years and 209 days. Associate Justice John Rutledge served the shortest, four months. The oldest to serve the court was Oliver Wendell Holmes, who retired at age ninety.

In 1789, the salary was $3,500 for justices, and $4,000 for the chief justice; today the justices are paid $164,100 and the chief justice, $171,500.

Each day that the court convenes, it holds a private conference in which the "conference handshake" is conducted. This nineteenth-century tradition began with Chief Justice Melville W. Fuller, who asked that each justice shake hands with each of the other eight to remind them that, despite differences of opinion, they share a common purpose: to uphold the Constitution of the United States of America.

Ms. Smith Comes to Washington: Women Senators and Representatives

In 1920—after seventy-two years of pleading, demonstrating, and arguing, American women won the right to vote with the passage of the Nineteenth Amendment.

The struggle forged new alliances. Black orator and self-taught publisher Frederick Douglass, a freed slave, was hugely influential in turning attention to women's right to vote, even though black men and women in many areas would not have that right for decades to come. Black women such as Sojourner Truth, Harriet Forten Purvis, Margaretta Forten, Caroline Remond Putnam, Josephine St. Pierre Ruffin, Ida B. Wells-Barnett, Mary Church Terrell, and Adella Hunt Logan also worked for the suffragist cause.

Interestingly, a woman was elected to the House of Representatives without the nationally decreed right to vote in her own election: Jeannette Rankin of Montana was elected in 1917.

One of the leaders of the campaign was Susan B. Anthony, who cast an illegal vote in the presidential election of 1872, for which she was promptly arrested, tried, and fined $100. She refused to pay. Following her arrest she gave a now-famous address that included these stirring lines:

Friends and fellow citizens: I stand before you tonight under indictment for the alleged crime of having voted at the last presidential election, without having a lawful right to vote. It shall be my work this evening to prove to you that in thus voting, I not only committed no crime, but, instead, simply exercised my citizen's rights, guaranteed to me and all United States citizens by the National Constitution, beyond the power of any state to deny. . . .

It was we, the people; not we, the white male citizens; nor yet we, the male citizens; but we, the whole people, who formed the Union. And we formed it, not to give the blessings of liberty, but to secure them; not to the half of ourselves and the half of our posterity, but to the whole people—women as well as men. And it is a downright mockery to talk to women of their enjoyment of the blessings of liberty while they are denied the use of the only means of securing them provided by this democratic-republican government—the ballot. . . .

The only question left to be settled now is: Are women persons? And I hardly believe any of our opponents will have the hardihood to say they are not. Being persons, then, women are citizens; and no state has a right to make any law, or to enforce any old law, that shall abridge their priv-

ileges or immunities. Hence, every discrimination against women in the constitutions and laws of the several states is today null and void, precisely as is every one against Negroes.

Anthony, who died in 1906, never lived to see her efforts realized. Fourteen years later, in August 1920, the Nineteenth Amendment to the U.S. Constitution was finally ratified, and women were given the right to vote.

Since Jeanette's Rankin's election, the picture continues to improve: 185 women have been elected to the House of Representatives, which today is much more of a "representation" of what constitutes the population, including blacks, Hispanics, Asians, and people of other national, cultural, and religious backgrounds.

Women have also taken their rightful place in the U.S. Senate, beginning on November 21, 1922, when Rebecca Latimer Felton of Georgia became the first to take the oath of office. Because of her active careers in politics and journalism, the eighty-seven-year-old Felton was appointed to fill a vacancy but served just two days.

Hattie Wyatt Caraway of Arkansas was the first woman to be elected to the Senate. After her husband, U.S. Senator Thaddeus Caraway, died, she was appointed to serve out the remainder of his term. She won reelection on her own in 1932 and 1938, and she served through 1945.

As of 2001, thirty-one women have served in the U.S. Senate, and thirteen serve at this time. We are proud of them all.

OUR SYMBOLS

This flag which we honor and under which we serve is the emblem of the unity of our power, our thought and purpose as a nation.

—Woodrow Wilson

Symbols of Freedom

During the War of Independence, Americans planted poplars and other trees, hung flags on them and "a cap of liberty" as symbols of growing freedom. Through the years, we have placed new and different symbols in our lexicon of freedom, and each has a unique and special meaning.

THE BALD EAGLE

The image of the magnificent American bald eagle graces our coins, our president's flag, the flags of several states, our military insignia, our postage stamps, and more. The eagle (scientific name: *Haliaeetus leucocephalus*, "sea eagle with a white head") was named our national bird in 1782, despite the campaign waged by Benjamin Franklin to elevate that other native bird, the wild turkey, to this lofty position. Congress chose the eagle, however, believing it to be as strong, determined, and brave as America itself.

Adult male bald eagles are three feet from head to tail, weigh seven to ten pounds, and have a wingspan of about six and one-half feet. Females are larger, up to fourteen pounds; they also have a wider wingspan, up to eight feet. Eagles can fly as fast as thirty miles per hour, they mate for life, and some live to the age of thirty.

Eagles once thrived on cliffsides and in the forests, where they fished in clean waters. As civilization encroached on the eagle's natural habitats, the great bird's survival became threatened, until at one point only 450 remained to be counted. On July 4, 1976, the bald eagle was officially recognized as an endangered species. The U.S. Fish and Wildlife Service established a large and successful breeding colony at its Patuxent Wildlife Research Center in Maryland. One result of this success is that today there are about ten times the eagle nesting pairs (4,500) than there were in the early 1960s.

The American bald eagle, its flight symbolic of the freedom we enjoy, is once more flying high and vigilant across our skies. We are proud of its survival.

THE LIBERTY BELL

The bell we call Liberty has a long and interesting history. The first version was ordered from the famous Whitechapel Foundry in London, where it was designed and cast by master founder Thomas Lester.

The magnificent bell, then called the State House bell, made its long journey from Great Britain to America only to sustain a crack while being hung, before it was ever rung. It was twice recast at a local foundry, but neither version was satisfactory, and both cracked. They sounded fine, though, and from 1753 until the Revolutionary War, one of these huge bells was rung to toll mourning

Proclaim liberty throughout all the land unto all the inhabitants thereof—Lev. XXV, v.x. By order of the Assembly of the Province of Pensylvania for the State House in Philada.

—Inscription on the Liberty Bell

for statesmen, to protest taxation, to mark important events and celebrate good tidings. One rang July 8, 1776, to announce the first public reading of the Declaration of Independence.

During our fight against the British, the bell was called the Bell of the Revolution, which soon evolved into Old Independence. The Liberty Bell got its current name in the 1840s, when supporters of the American Anti-Slavery Society used the bell as a symbol for its cause to proclaim "liberty for all." In 1846, it acquired the familiar "zigzag" crack upon being rung for Washington's birthday.

The City of Philadelphia purchased the bell from the State of Pennsylvania in 1816, and from 1876 through 1915 it was displayed throughout the country. It was paraded through the streets of Philadelphia during World War I and during World War II. To preserve the fragile symbol, one stroke for each letter in the words INDEPENDENCE and LIBERTY were tapped upon the bell with a rubber mallet.

The Liberty Bell now rests in a special showcase, the Independence Pavilion, on Philadelphia's famed Market Street, near Independence Hall. Every Fourth of July, the bell is "rung" with a careful tap.

How to Fold an American Flag

FOLDING THE AMERICAN FLAG
WITH RESPECT AND HONOR

The American flag is not only a banner and symbol of the United States, it is a sacred object. It should be handled in a precisely prescribed manner.

- Lowering the flag from its pole, take care that *no* part of the flag touches the ground.

- Hold the flag waist high with another person so that it is parallel to the ground.

- Fold the lower half of the stripe section lengthwise over the field of stars, holding the bottom and top edges securely.

- Fold the flag lengthwise again, with the blue field on the *outside*.

- Make a triangular fold by bringing the striped corner of the folded end to meet the open top edge of the flag.

- Turn the outer end point inward, parallel to the open end, to form a second triangle.

- The triangular folding is repeated until the entire length of the flag is folded down to the size of a tricornered hat.

- When completely folded, only a triangular blue field of stars should be visible.

The tricorner shape is to remind us of the hats worn by American soldiers during the War for Independence. The red-and-white stripes are wrapped around the blue, as light folds into night. Our Armed Forces stand guard over folded flags as a tribute to our nation's honored dead, and the flag is brought out each morning at reveille to fly as a symbol of resurrection.

The Statue of Liberty

Whether a first-time visitor or a local resident of New York City, when you gaze out over New York Harbor you will be greeted by a lady whose presence is majestic, commanding, comforting, welcoming. Towering above us, she symbolizes freedom, opportunity, and liberty. She is the Statue of Liberty, and in the eyes of millions around the world, she is America.

The idea for the Statue of Liberty was born when France wanted to acknowledge the American people for the friendship that began during the American Revolution. The project—a joint effort between the two countries—took years, missed the actual centennial date (1876), and involved thousands of people on both sides of the Atlantic in the construction, shipment, assemblage, and underwriting of her placement. No one looking at the magnificent lady can ever doubt that the effort was worth it.

The French commissioned sculptor Frederic Auguste Batholdi to design the statue and Alexandre Gustave Eiffel (of the famous Paris tower) to design the massive iron pylon and secondary skeletal framework that allows the statue's "skin" to move independently yet stand upright.

The statue arrived aboard the French frigate *Isère* in June of 1885, the 350 individual pieces packaged in 214 crates. It took a frigate to carry it because of the weight: 31 tons of copper and 125 tons of steel. The reassembly took four months to complete.

The Statue of Liberty is 151 feet 1 inch high from base to torch. From the ground to the tip of the torch, it stands 305 feet 1 inch. To reach the crown, you must climb 354 steps. The crown has twenty-five windows, which symbolize the gemstones found on earth, and its seven rays represent the seven seas and seven continents of the world. The tablet in her left hand reads "July 4, 1776" in roman numerals. Joseph Pulitzer's *New York World* financed the 27,000-ton concrete pedestal on which the statue stands.

Lady Liberty was formally dedicated on October 28, 1886. She remains the most recognizable symbol of freedom and justice in the world. The poem by Emma Lazarus at her feet speaks eloquently to immigrants and native-born Americans alike:

THE NEW COLOSSUS

Not like the brazen giant of Greek fame,
With conquering limbs astride from land to land;
Here at our sea-washed, sunset gates shall stand

A mighty woman with a torch, whose flame
Is the imprisoned lightning, and her name
Mother of Exiles. From her beacon-hand
Glows world-wide welcome; her mild eyes command
The air-bridged harbor that twin cities frame.

"Keep, ancient lands, your storied pomp!" cries she
With silent lips. "Give me your tired, your poor,
Your huddled masses yearning to breathe free,
The wretched refuse of your teeming shore.
Send these, the homeless, tempest-tossed to me.
I lift my lamp beside the golden door!"

Ellis Island: Gateway to America

For more than sixty years, Ellis Island was the place where most immigrants first set foot in the United States of America. Here, they were "processed," receiving their papers, medical examinations as necessary, and given that most precious item of all: freedom.

From 1892 to 1954 more than twelve million immigrants passed through this island in New York Harbor. The first was a fifteen-year-old Irish girl, Annie Moore, and the last was a Norwegian merchant seaman, Arne Peterssen. They came, like most immigrants do, because of political instability, restrictive religious laws, or a deteriorating economy in their homelands. Many of their personal possessions, along with the full story of the waves of nineteenth-century and early twentieth-century immigration through this portal, can now be seen in the newly refurbished Ellis Island Immigration Museum.

The museum is the result of the largest historic restoration in U.S. history. Begun in 1984 and completed on September 10, 1990, the project was funded by donations made to the Statue of Liberty—

Ellis Island Foundation. Directing the drive for funds was the son of Italian immigrants, Lee Iacocca, former chairman of Chrysler Corporation. Today the museum, like the Statue of Liberty, operates under the auspices of the National Park Service.

In the museum, descendants of the millions who passed through Ellis Island can relive the experience, view photos and memorabilia, and marvel at the spirit of their forebears.

"The Star-Spangled Banner"

Lawyer and amateur poet Francis Scott Key (1779–1843) was so moved by the sight of the U.S. flag waving amid the British cannon fire over Baltimore's Fort McHenry on September 14, 1814, that he wrote the words that became our national anthem.

In the early hours of September 13, 1814, the British began a twenty-five-hour battle that ended at about 1 A.M. the following day. Key, at the side of two other Americans. Col. John Skinner and Dr. William Beanes, whom he helped to get released from British captivity, watched the battle with hope that Fort McHenry would not fall. The early dawn brought an eerie silence as, they later discovered, the British forces had retreated.

At daybreak Key, heartened by the still-waving flag, dashed off a poem on the back of a letter he had in his pocket. The poem was printed and distributed in and around Baltimore as "Defence of Fort M'Henry" (two broadsides have survived), and on September 20, 1814, the *Baltimore Patriot* started a wave of reprints in newspapers throughout the colonies. The poem was first performed as a song in Baltimore by a local actor. Referring to the poem as "The

Star-Spangled Banner," he sang the words to the melody of a traditional hymn known as "To Anacreon in Heaven," whose composer is unknown.

The flag that inspired Key's poem is now in the Smithsonian Institution's Museum of American History. Due to its fragility, it is exposed for viewing for just a few moments every hour. Fort McHenry is now a national monument The magnificent flag, made at the request of Major George Armistead, who asked for a flag "so big the British would have no trouble seeing it from a distance," was the creation of Mary Young Pickersgill and her thirteen-year-old daughter Caroline, who skillfully stitched together the thirty-by-forty-foot flag for the then-exhorbitant sum of $405.90.

The letter with the original poem on it is now owned by the Maryland Historical Society. Another copy, with Key's writing, is in the Library of Congress.

"The Star-Spangled Banner" officially became our national anthem on March 3, 1931. We sing it with pride.

THE STAR-SPANGLED BANNER

Oh, say, can you see, by the dawn's early light,
What so proudly we hailed at the twilight's last gleaming?
Whose broad stripes and bright stars, thro' the perilous fight
O'er the ramparts we watched, were so gallantly streaming.
And the rockets red glare, the bombs bursting in air,
Gave proof through the night that our flag was still there.
Oh, say, does that star-spangled banner yet wave
O'er the land of the free and the home of the brave?

On the shore dimly seen, thro' the mists of the deep,
Where the foe's haughty host in dread silence reposes,
What is that which the breeze, o'er the towering steep,
As it fitfully blows, half conceals, half discloses?

Now it catches the gleam of the morning's first beam,
In full glory reflected, now shines on the stream;
'Tis the star-spangled banner: Oh, long may it wave
O'er the land of the free and the home of the brave.

And where is that band who so vauntingly swore
That the havoc of war and the battle's confusion
A home and a country should leave us no more?
Their blood has wash'd out their foul footstep's pollution.
No refuge could save the hireling and slave
From the terror of flight or the gloom of the grave,
And the star-spangled banner in triumph doth wave
O'er the land of the free and the home of the brave.

Oh, thus be it ever when free men shall stand,
Between their loved homes and the war's desolation;
Blest with vict'ry and peace, may the heav'n-rescued land
Praise the Power that has made and preserved us as a nation.
Then conquer we must, when our cause is just,
And this be our motto: "In God is our trust";
And the star-spangled banner in triumph shall wave
O'er the land of the free and the home of the brave.

Songs That Stir the Heart

Our patriotic songs are etched in our minds and hearts. "My Country 'tis of Thee" and "America the Beautiful" are perhaps the ones we love best.

"My Country 'tis of Thee" was written in 1832 by Samuel Francis Smith (1808–1895). Smith attended both Harvard University and Andover Theological Seminary and spent his life as a minister teaching and writing and editing books, essays, poetry, and songs ("Rock of Ages" and many others). His famous poem, like many of that era, was set to a hymn, in this case "Thesaurus Musicus," written in 1744.

MY COUNTRY 'TIS OF THEE

My country, 'tis of thee,
Sweet land of liberty,
Of thee I sing.
Land where my fathers died,
Land of the pilgrims' pride,
From every mountainside
Let freedom ring.

My native country, thee,
Land of the noble free,
Thy name I love.
I love thy rocks and rills,
Thy woods and templed hills.
My heart with rapture thrills
Like that above.

Let music swell the breeze,
And ring from all the trees
Sweet freedom's song;
Let mortal tongues awake,
Let all that breathe partake:
Let rocks their silence break,
The sound prolong.

Our fathers' God, to thee,
Author of liberty,
To thee we sing;
Long may our land be bright
With freedom's holy light;
Protect us by thy might,
Great God, our King.

★ ★ ★

Katharine Lee Bates (1859–1929) a poet, English professor, and a Massachusetts native, wrote the words to "America the Beautiful."

A graduate of Wellesley College, she studied at Oxford. In 1893, she made an ambitious journey across the states from her native Falmouth to Chicago's World's Fair to Colorado, where she traveled up Pike's Peak to view Colorado Springs from the 14,110-foot summit. She wrote of the day and its experience that "our sojourn on the peak remains in memory hardly more than one ecstatic gaze. It was then and there as I was looking out over the sea-like expanse of fertile country spreading away so far under those ample skies, that the opening lines of the hymn floated into my mind."

She published her poem in *The Congregationalist* (her father was a minister) in 1895, and it was set to a hymn written by Silas G. Pratt in 1897. More than sixty other musical tunes have been used with it over the years, but the one most widely accepted and the one used today was Samuel A. Ward's *Materna*. Bates wrote to a friend, "That the hymn has gained . . . such a hold as it has upon our people, is clearly due to the fact that Americans are at heart idealists, with a fundamental faith in human brotherhood."

AMERICA THE BEAUTIFUL

O beautiful for spacious skies,
For amber waves of grain,
For purple mountain majesties
Above the fruited plain.
America! America!
God shed His grace on thee
And crown thy good with brotherhood
From sea to shining sea.

O beautiful for pilgrim feet
Whose stern impassioned stress
A thoroughfare for freedom beat
Across the wilderness.
America! America!
God mend thine every flaw,
Confirm thy soul in self-control,
Thy liberty in law.

O beautiful for heroes proved
In liberating strife,
Who more than self their country loved,
And mercy more than life.

America! America!
May God thy gold refine
Till all success be nobleness,
And every gain divine.

O beautiful for patriot dream
That sees beyond the years.
Thine alabaster cities gleam
Undimmed by human tears.
America! America!
God shed His grace on thee,
And crown thy good with brotherhood
From sea to shining sea.

OUR LAND

This land is your land, this land is my land,
From California to the New York Island,
From the Redwood Forest to the Gulf stream waters,
This land was made for you and me...

     —Woody Guthrie
      "This Land Is Your Land"

Engineering Marvels of American Genius:
Bridges, Tunnels, and Dams

How can we transport people from one end of this vast country to another, across waterways and mountains, deserts and forests? How high can we build? How far under the ocean or earth can we dig? What materials can we develop to make our goals a reality?

These and thousands more questions were asked by every engineer, designer, architect, and government agency that has participated in the design, development, funding, construction, and maintenance of our greatest engineering marvels: bridges, tunnels, and dams. We're proud of them all; here are just a few of the grandest:

THE VERRAZANO NARROWS BRIDGE, BROOKLYN, NEW YORK

When Giovanni da Verrazano first sailed through New York Harbor in 1524, his wooden boat was one of the engineering miracles of that era, enabling him to travel from Italy to explore the New World in a matter of months. Imagine his astonishment if he had been present 440 years later to see the longest suspension bridge in the world open on November 21, 1964. Spanning 4,260 feet between towers 693 feet high, the Verrazano stretches across the upper New York Bay to connect Brooklyn to Staten Island. The towers are so high and so far apart that the curvature of the earth was a critical factor in their construction—requiring that they be built an additional $1\frac{1}{58}$ inches apart. Today the Verrazano is the world's sixth-longest bridge.

The Verrazano was designed by Othmar Ammann (who was also involved in the design of four other huge New York bridges) and built for a cost of about $325 million, the most ever spent (to that time) on a bridge project. The cost, originally borne by the Triborough Bridge and Tunnel Authority, has been recouped with public funds and toll charges.

THE BROOKLYN BRIDGE, NEW YORK

Near the Verrazano is another spectacular suspension bridge that is nearly a century older. The Brooklyn Bridge is 6,016 feet (1.14 miles) end to end, and was the first to use pneumatic caissons and steel cable. The bridge had been under discussion for more than sixty years before it was built, and when it was finally completed in 1883, it cost a then-astonishing $15 million.

Its towers are 276 feet 6 inches high. and the bridge runs 135 feet above water. The East River span is 1595 feet, six inches long, and the support land span is 930 feet long. Each steel cable is made up of 5,434 wires that are each 3,578 feet 6 inches long.

The designer was Wilhelm Hildenbrand, but it was wire manufacturer John A. Roebling who provided strong steel-wire cable that made the bridge possible—at a time when steel was so new it was distrusted. (Iron was then the metal of choice.) The cast-steel wires were spun on the site. The construction, which began in January 1870, was exhausting and very dangerous for the bridge workers, because so little was then known about the causes of caisson disease (the bends). Nearly thirty workers died; John Roebling died from lockjaw as a result of an injury, and his son Washington, who took over the project, developed caisson disease and completed the work as an invalid. From a window in Brooklyn, he watched the site through telescope. His wife, Emily, acted as his daily emissary, visiting the construction site and relaying his instructions.

Almost fourteen years after the first excavation was made, the Brooklyn Bridge opened on May 24, 1883, to welcome 15,300 pedestrians paying a toll of a penny, and 1,800 vehicles paying a nickel to cross. Today more than 150,000 vehicles and about 4,000 pedestrians and bicyclists cross the Brooklyn Bridge each day, toll free.

THE GOLDEN GATE BRIDGE, SAN FRANCISCO

Each thrilling trip across the Golden Gate brings a completely different vista: rainbows, fog, clear sunlit days, the mystery and magic of gold lamps lighting the crossing at night. Chief Engineer Joseph B. Strauss certainly had a vision, but even he could not have imagined his creation would become one of the nation's favorite structural wonders.

Though its orange-vermilion color, International Orange, blends in with the span's natural setting and sometimes appears golden, the bridge was named for the three-mile-long Golden Gate Strait that lies between the Pacific Ocean and San Francisco Bay. Each tower has 600,000 rivets, and the fabricated steel came from Bethlehem Steel plants in Trenton, New Jersey; Sparrows Point, Maryland; and Bethlehem, Pottstown, and Steelton, Pennsylvania. The steel was transported in sections, first by rail to Philadelphia, then shipped through the Panama Canal to San Francisco. The bridge has been seismically retrofitted to protect it from earthquake damage. Daily maintenance involves seventeen ironworkers and thirty-eight painters who work in fog, powerful winds, and biting sea air, from the top of the towers to the underbellies of the gate, to repair damage and corrosion.

The Golden Gate, which took four years to build, opened to the public on May 28, 1937. At the time it was the longest span in the world, 4,200 feet. Today it is the seventh. The bridge now has six traffic lanes, and the current toll is $3.

HOOVER DAM

A National Historic Landmark, Hoover Dam is a civil engineering wonder. In 1905 the continual flooding of the Colorado River into the Imperial Valley of California became so intense that it created a completely new body of water: the Salton Sea. Designed to control the destructive flooding, the dam was championed by conservationist-engineer Herbert Hoover, the thirty-first president and a former Secretary of Commerce. "Civilization advances with the practical application of knowledge in such structures. . . ." he said of the dam. "The spread of its values in [support of] human happiness is beyond computation."

Located about thirty miles southeast of Las Vegas, the Hoover Dam spans the Colorado River between Arizona and Nevada. The monolithic concrete marvel weighs more than 6 million tons, rises up 726.4 feet from its foundation, and contains more than 3.25

million cubic yards of concrete. The maximum water pressure at its base is 45,000 pounds per square foot.

Despite its mammoth size and dramatic engineering, which involved cooling concrete with ice during critical time periods, Hoover Dam took less than five years to construct. It would have been an ambitious project at any time, but in the Great Depression, the dam did more than control flooding and increase the clean-water supply. It also employed thousands of workers who would have otherwise been unlikely to find employment. For more than six decades Hoover Dam has done exactly what its namesake engineer-president promised it would: "The waters of this great river, instead of being wasted in the sea, will now be brought into use by man."

CHESAPEAKE BAY BRIDGE-TUNNEL

This remarkable feat of engineering crosses both over and under open waters where the Chesapeake Bay meets the Atlantic Ocean. It links Virginia and the Delmarva Peninsula abutting Delaware, Maryland, and Virginia, and cuts almost one hundred miles off the trip between the city of Virginia Beach and points just north of Wilmington, Delaware. The total length, including approach roads, is 23 miles; it spans water that ranges from 25 to 100 feet deep. It was designed by Sverdrup & Parcel, consulting engineers, and Sverdrup Civil, Inc., both of Maryland Heights, Missouri.

The Chesapeake Bay Bridge-Tunnel opened to considerable

fanfare on April 15, 1964, and since then more than 67 million passenger and commercial vehicles have crossed it. And just to put the cherry on the sundae, a parallel crossing project was built (without tax dollars!) for four-lane traffic in the 1990s. Among the astonishing components of this project are twelve miles of low-level trestle, two one-mile-long underwater tunnels, two bridges, two miles of causeway, and four manmade islands of about 10 acres each, located at the end of the two tunnels.

Tunnels are a different kind of engineering miracle. Building them requires humans to burrow like gophers, risk collapse of heavy earth, and think like miners in the dark underground. We have learned how to blast through mountains (using dyamite and rock drills invented in the 1840s), bore through rock (with tunnel borers invented only in the 1970s), and dig under waterways (the old-fashioned way, using manpower and huge mechanical shoveling machines). Recent technological advances have made it easier to create tunnels to accommodate subways, high-speed trains, and vehicular traffic and transoceanic fiber optic cable.

All this mechanical and technological progress has produced such phenomenal American achievements as the New York City subway system, the Lincoln and Holland tunnels under the Hudson River, the Detroit-Windsor Tunnel under the Detroit River (linking the United States with Canada); the Arrowhead East Tunnel bored through a California mountain; and the newest subway tunnels in Washington, D.C., and Los Angeles.

From Sea to Shining Sea

A poor woman lived all her life in the rugged hills of West Virginia, an area with land impervious to seed or tireless effort. Asked why she continued to live there instead of moving where she could grow food or get a better job, she said, "Oh, it's so pretty when the dogwood blooms in springtime."

The beauty of nature is found in every state of the union, from the exotic flowers of Hawaii to the bluegrass of Kentucky to the rocky shores of Maine. We are blessed with such variety that our land could be a textbook for a geographer: stately redwoods stories high; mighty rivers, placid lakes, Niagara Falls; the fiery foliage of a New England autumn, the rich soil of Nebraska wheat fields, rows of corn in Iowa; fruits and vegetables grown in so many states, especially California (which produces more than any other *country* in the world).

Thanks to the efforts of President Theodore Roosevelt, John Muir, the Sierra Club, and many other conservationists and lovers of nature, we have a system of national and state parks that bring peace and recreational opportunities to campers, hikers, and everyone who enjoys the grandeur of nature. Like Yellowstone and Yosemite national parks, the Grand Canyon attracts visitors from around the world.

The blue-green of our mountains invite exploration and appreciation: the Grand Tetons, the Rockies, the Ozarks, and the Blue Ridge, the Sierras, the Smoky Mountains, Alleghenies, Berkshires, Catskills, and more. We have the majestic Mount Shasta, Mount McKinley, Mount Whitney, and Mount Rainier. Each has its unique flora and fauna, but one common attribute is that they are ours to enjoy, treasure, and protect.

The choices of natural splendor are so vast: the stillness of the prairie at dusk; the brilliant pink and blue sunsets over the deserts of the Southwest; the mighty thunder of waves along the beaches of the Pacific and Atlantic oceans; the gloomy glory of the Georgia swamps or the Florida Everglades. We can swim, ski, sail, and paddle along the mighty Mississippi, fish in local streams and lakes, canoe down rapids, hang out along beaches, or just sit and think at any one of thousands of creeks, rivers, ponds, bays, and inlets—from the chilly Great Lakes to the seemingly bottomless Lake Tahoe.

The beauty of America is as simple and as elegant as a wildflower, as endless as the horizon over oceans. The beauty of American is as deep as the thickest forest or as open as the vast expanse of our deserts.

As the Native Americans know, Beauty is all around us, beside us, above us, beneath us. We are pledged to be her caretaker.

Here are just a few more of the many other natural wonders that are a source of pride to us all:

Mauna Loa
Sequoia National Park
Klamath Basin National
  Wildlife Refuge
Bryce Canyon
The Green Mountains
The Missouri River
Eureka Springs
Ouachita National Forest
Havasu Canyon
Petrified Forest/Painted Desert
Monument Valley
Salt River Canyon

Chiricahua National
  Park
The Rio Grande
The Susquehanna River
The Great Salt Lake
Lake Placid
Lake Champlain
Atlantic and Pacific beaches
The Gulf of Mexico
The Mojave Desert
Cape Cod
Meteor Crater
The Florida Keys

OUR PEOPLE

I hear America singing, the varied carols I hear,
Those of mechanics, each one singing his as it should
   be blithe and strong,
The carpenter singing his as he measures his plank
   or beam,
The mason singing his as he makes ready for work,
   or leaves off work...

> —Walt Whitman
> "I Hear America Singing"

We Serve and Protect

From the smallest township to the largest municipality, America has a system of law enforcement and protection services to handle emergencies, crimes, and natural or man-made disasters. Thanks to increasing professionalism, advanced training, and sophisticated technology, our law enforcement agencies are more effective than ever. DNA testing, computerized fingerprinting, and interstate data tracking are some of the high-tech tools used to identify and convict perpetrators.

The Center for Disease Control in Atlanta protects the safety and health of our people living at home or traveling abroad. The CDC supplies education and information to prevent or control disease and environmental health threats.

The Secret Service provides personal security to our president and vice president and their families and to visiting dignitaries.

The Federal Bureau of Investigation (FBI) protects the country from terrorist activities, against invasive foreign intelligence, and assists local and international agencies in enforcing federal laws. The Central Intelligence Agency (CIA) evaluates intelligence information that may threaten national security. The CIA reports to the president through the director of Central Intelligence. Both agencies are accountable to the people through the National Security Committee, which reports to both houses of the Congress.

Our police departments have created powerful community outreach programs to teach self-defense to everyone (especially women and the elderly), establish Neighborhood Watch Programs, and they use innovative, even entertaining approaches to teaching children about traffic safety, how to respond to emergencies, and how to steer clear of drug use and crime. It's not an easy job, but our men and women police officers work hard every day to help us create stronger, safer communities.

And should we find ourselves in serious trouble—lost on a mountain trail, floundering in dangerous waters, or looking for shelter in a bad snowstorm—our advanced search-and-rescue teams will often get us out safely. Park Rangers protect our national and state parks, educate visitors about safety, and can help those who are lost or in danger.

Our Coast Guard rescues sailors and boats caught up in storms or tides or adrift in our oceans. And all the branches of the military are prepared to serve in a multitude of ways far too numerous to list here.

In a natural disaster such as an earthquake, flood, tornado, and hurricane or forest fire, the National Guard helps people find safety, manages traffic, and guards property. Both volunteer county and municipal firefighters perform the heroic every day: They climb trees and tall buildings to rescue indifferent cats, frightened children, or fragile adults. They teach us and our children the rules of fire safety that may one day save us. They train arduously and continue to learn new ways to protect and serve. They remain as sentries on the ashes of great fires to ensure that sparks do not rise again.

They rescue us from the aftermath of accidents and disasters. They are called upon to put their lives on the line to save ours.

To all these dedicated men and women in our cities and in our parks, along our shores and in our mountains, America is proud of you, grateful for you, beholden to you.

We Are a Nation of Volunteers

In every disaster or emergency, the people of America demonstrate their true sense of community.

Floods, fires, earthquakes, hurricanes, tornadoes, crashes, catastrophes of all sorts bring out our generosity, in funds, hours of labor, and dedication to the needs of others. Within the first fifteen minutes of the national telethon after the terrorist attacks on New York City and Washington, D.C., more than 300,000 people called in donations that contributed to an astonishing $150 million dollars raised within just a few hours. And the money continued to pour in, easing the anguish and rebuilding for the future.

On September 11, 2001, medical personnel rushed to hospitals, leaving personal interests behind, to take care of the injured. Mental-health workers helped children and adults deal with the resulting panic, fear, stress, and emotional trauma. People donated blood and companies and individuals donated goods, services, and food. Volunteer agencies provided support services and direct aid.

All of it mattered. All of it counted. Yet the tireless workers volunteering to clear away the detritus of the attack, to venture into the unstable and dangerous heaps of rubble answered to a gut response that said, "I can help, and I will." Yet, when asked about their service, these volunteers inevitably say they receive more than they give.

Doing, giving, sharing because one *can* is an American ideal expressed every day, not just during crises. How else can we explain the constancy and dedication of volunteer fire companies, aides in classrooms and in hospitals, of people building shelters for the homeless?

Perhaps no other gift we give matters as much as a volunteer's visit. To take the time to rock a baby, hold the hand of the dying, entertain a hospitalized child, or comfort the bereaved is to give in a way that has no price.

American volunteers aren't just there when tragedy strikes, either. They serve as guides who enthusiastically share the joy and thrill of music, art, dance, theater with youngsters and adults. Volunteers bring meals on wheels, bookmobiles, and home and health care to the housebound. Volunteers steer committees and chair meetings that raise funds, register people to vote, teach a disabled person the thrill of riding a horse or playing on a basketball court.

Volunteers help at sports events from kids' soccer leagues to the Special Olympics, offer support and counsel to youth groups, senior citizens homes, and caregivers of the chronically or terminally ill. Volunteers aid the traveler and the visitor in our parks, zoos, and public monuments. Volunteers give of their time, their money, their spirit.

Volunteers are the heartbeat of America, doing good for their fellow citizens wherever there is need for consolation, for advocacy, for sharing joy.

THE PEACE CORPS: AMERICANS HELPING TO BUILD A BETTER WORLD

On January 20, 1961, in his inaugural address, President John F. Kennedy challenged a new generation of Americans to join "a grand and global alliance . . . to fight tyranny, poverty, disease, and war."

The challenge was met nine months later when Congress, following an executive order by Kennedy, authorized the establishment of the Peace Corps to "promote world peace and friendship" throughout the world, to promote better understanding of Americans on the part of those served, and to help us better understand other peoples.

R. Sargent Shriver was appointed the first director, and more than 7,000 Peace Corps volunteers signed up in the next few years. At its peak, the Peace Corps was 15,000-strong. Over four decades, 163,000 volunteers and trainees have done good works and deeds in 135 countries. Currently 7,300 are working in seventy-two countries. Carol Bellamy was the first returned volunteer to direct the Corps and is now executive director of UNICEF. The most recent volunteer to direct is Josephine K. "Jody" Olsen, the former executive director of the Council for International Exchange of Scholars, which manages the Fulbright Scholar program.

Peace Corps volunteers have done whatever needed to be done, which included digging wells; building irrigation and sewage systems; constructing housing, hospitals, and schools; teaching reading, hygiene, and prenatal and infant care; demonstrating better techniques in farming and health care; even helping craftspeople learn how to export and sell their wares.

Among the veterans of the Corps are such accomplished individuals as these:

Leon Dash, Pulitzer Prize-winning journalist of the *Washington Post* and recently appointed Swanlund Chair for journalism and Afro-American Studies at the University of Illinois at Urbana (Kenya, 1969–1970)

Taylor Hackford, producer of *An Officer and a Gentleman* (Bolivia 1968–1969)

Gordon Radley, president of Lucasfilms Ltd. (Malawi, 1968–1970)

Bob Vila, of *This Old House* (Panama, 1969–1970)

Bob Becklel, CNN's *Crossfire* political analyst (Philippines, (1971–1972)

Paul Theroux, author of *The Mosquito Coast* and many other books (Malawi, 1963–1965)

Senator Chistopher Dodd, Connecticut (Dominican Republic, 1966–1968)

U.S. Representatives Sam Farr, California (Colombia, 1964–1966); Mike Honda, California (El Salvador, 1965–1967); James Walsh,

New York, (Nepal, 1970–1972); Christopher Shays, Connecticut (Fiji, 1968–1970); Thomas Petri, Wisconsin (Somalia, 1966–1967); Tony Hall, Ohio (Thailand, 1966–1967); and Governor Robert Taft, Ohio (Tanzania, 1963–1965)

Michael McCaskey, chairman of the board, Chicago Bears (Ethiopia, 1965–1967)

Donna Shalala, president of Miami University and former Secretary of Health and Human Services (Iran, 1962–1964)

Carl Pope, executive director of the Sierra Club (India, 1967–1969)

Robert Haas, chairman of the board, Levi Strauss (Ivory Coast, 1964–1966)

The Peace Corps also provided early experience in diplomacy to at least four Americans who became ambassadors:

Ambassador to Honduras Frank Almaguer (Belize, 1967–1969); Ambassador to Kenya Johnnie Carson (Tanzania, 1965–1968); Ambassador to Indonesia Robert Gelbard (Bolivia, 1964–1968); and Ambassador to Paraguay David Greenlee (Bolivia, 1965–1967).

They are some of the thousands of Americans who answered President Kennedy's call. These volunteers brought their can-do attitude back to the United States to serve in business, education, government, foreign service, philanthropy, and the arts.

Today's Peace Corps is as ambitious as ever and more diverse. The average age of Corps volunteers is currently about twenty-five, and the oldest is eighty-two, proving that you're never too old to share your experience and your knowledge with those in need. The Peace Corps: Americans helping the world to be a better place.

HELPING OUR NEIGHBORS IN NEED

From barn raising to fund-raising, the tradition of Americans helping Americans has been a constant in our history. Good neighbors care about one another just as family members do. We bring food to the bereaved and the ill, watch out for our neighbors' children, call to check on the elderly or infirm, and provide billions of dollars to support thousands of charitable organizations. Here are just a handful of the countless organizations that exemplify the American spirit of volunteerism.

THE AMERICAN RED CROSS.   When disaster strikes—natural or man-made—the familiar red-and-white vans carrying paramedics, nurses, blood, and food and clothing will be there. At home and abroad, the Red Cross is there. In between crises, one of its most critical contributions is the collection of blood donations. Each year, the Red Cross collects 48 percent of the nation's blood supply. That's near 6.4 million units (or pints) during the fiscal year 2001 so far. Ordinarily it collects 13.2 million units each year. The holidays are the most critical time during noncrisis situations, so when you're making out your gift list, add "donate blood." Can't give blood? Donate time, energy, or funds. The American Red Cross is ready when needed because you care to give today.

THE UNITED WAY OF AMERICA.   Supports more than twenty-two different organizations that fund local community programs at a level second only to the federal government. Last year it raised more than $3 billion for food, clothing, and shelter; for counseling for trauma, for education; and for a variety of programs that help schools and families.

THE NATIONAL ASSOCIATION OF CHILDRENS HOSPITALS, INC. (NACH) and SHRINERS CHILDRENS HOSPITALS

Twenty-two Shriners Hospitals and more than one hundred childrens hospitals provide the finest medical treatment in the world for any child in need. Guilds, support groups, and community donations have given thousands of children the gift of life or the comfort of care during terminal stages of an illness. Volunteer efforts and donations help provide the medicine, therapy, treatment, surgery, and day-to-day attention seriously or chronically ill children. Just as important, these hospitals reach out to families, providing them with counseling, transportation, respite services, and accommodations for relatives who live too far away to commute. Shriners Hospitals are dedicated primarily to orthopedic and neuromusculoskeletal conditions and burn care. They are supported by the Shriners organization of Freemasons and their many fundraising projects. Childrens hospitals are supported by auxiliaries, guilds, and community support, and they treat children with everything, including blindness, disabilities, chronic or terminal illness, and injuries from accidents and burns. No child is turned away.

Childrens hospitals aim to improve children's health, education, safety, and security through child advocacy.

GOODWILL INDUSTRIES.   This organization helps people help themselves in ways that count. More than 84 percent of its income from retail sales in its 1,700 stores and other donations provide job training and career services to provide the disabled, those with special needs, and the disenfranchised with meaningful work. With 179 autonomous member groups in the U.S. and 36 international members in 25 countries, Goodwill serves nearly 400,000 people in employement and training programs.

THE MARCH OF DIMES.   Begun as the National Foundation for Infantile Paralysis by President Franklin Delano Roosevelt in 1938, the March of Dimes got its name when entertainer Eddie Cantor urged Americans to send dimes to the White House to help fund the president's campaign against infantile paralysis. In its sixty-three years, the organization has funded research for vaccines, therapies, in-utero surgery, and medical research that has helped prevent death and disabilities in babies. Research funding from the March of Dimes has contributed to such medical breakthroughs as Dr. Jonas Salk's polio vaccine, Dr. Albert Sabin's oral polio vaccine, the PKU (phenylketonuria) test to prevent one form of mental retardation, the use of surfactant to treat respiratory distress syndrome in premature infants, gene therapy, bone marrow transplants to prevent birth defects, and campaigns to inform pregnant women about stress management and the importance of folic acid and nutrition in preventing birth defects. Ten scientists funded by the organization have won the Nobel Prize.

MADD (MOTHERS AGAINST DRUNK DRIVING) has in twenty years helped make "designated driver" not only a part of our lexicon but a part of the responsibility of every host, restaurateur, and business that serves alcohol. They have successfully targeted teenagers to become aware of the need to not drink and drive. The group also has been instrumental in the passage of hundreds of laws throughout the country that make drinking and driving illegal, increase the public awareness of every citizen's responsibility to the rest of us, and raise the minimum driving age.

THE SALVATION ARMY was founded in England by a Christian convert named William Booth in 1865. Active on American shores today, it is both an evangelical and a community service organization. Its current mission is to help rebuild the parts of the Pentagon destroyed in the September 11 attack, and to continue its work nationally to support people in need with food, shelter, and job training.

MAKE-A-WISH FOUNDATION.   This organization has been granting the wishes of terminally and chronically ill children all across the country and many parts of the world since 1980. Whether it's a visit from a sports hero, a trip to Disneyland, or a chance to ride an airplane, the group answers the request for these children's special wishes.

MEALS ON WHEELS.   This community-based group has provided nutritious, hot meals daily to those housebound by age or infirmity, either free or on a sliding-scale basis. Cooks, drivers, and staff are volunteers, and thousands of restaurants, food suppliers, and growers provide food, backed monetary donations from community agencies and individuals. The original program was launched in England during World War II to help the elderly. The first American chapter was established in Philadelphia in 1954. It's been growing in this country by leaps and bounds, and chapters are now active in many large cities and small towns across this country.

FARM AID: SAVING THE HANDS THAT FEED US

In just sixteen years, Farm Aid concerts and volunteers have raised more than $15 million for more than 100 farm organizations, churches, and service agencies in forty-four states. This money funds emergency aid, legal assistance, and hotlines for farmers and their families. Program grants help promote outreach education, the development of long-term solutions for the problems unique to rural America, and allow organizations to build on the energy and know-how of family farmers everywhere.

Musicians Willie Nelson, John Mellencamp, and Neil Young formed Farm Aid in 1985 and have staged concerts each year, most recently in Noblesville, Indiana, in September 2001. The goal, Nelson says, is to keep family farms operating and solvent. The fight to save family farms isn't just about farmers, it's about making sure that there is a safe and healthy food supply for all of us. It's about jobs, from Main Street to Wall Street. It's about a better America.

HABITAT FOR HUMANITY

Founded twenty-five years ago by Millard and Linda Fuller, Habitat for Humanity is an ecumenical Christian ministry devoted to eliminating substandard housing throughout the world. Volunteers have helped to build more than 100,000 homes in 2,000 communities in more than 70 countries.

Former President Jimmy Carter and Rosalynn Carter have traveled the globe directly helping other countries participate in this program, and they have helped build hundreds of homes themselves. Oprah Winfrey's Angel Network has provided furnishings from major American suppliers; Laura and President George Bush helped build a home in August 2001 in Waco, Texas; and volunteers from every strata of American life have participated in this outstanding program.

American volunteers: We take pride in helping each other to lead better lives.

We Make Sacrifices

THE SUM OF WAR: THE DEAD, THE INJURED, THE MIA

The personal price of war is the loss of those we love. Ask any parent, sibling, spouse, friend. While we can understand that loss of life is the cruel price to pay for our freedoms, we as individuals often find the price extremely high. But generations of Americans have believed that the values of this nation were worth fighting for and, if necessary, dying for. We as a nation have been taught to love and defend freedom today, so that our children and our children's children will not have to make the ultimate sacrifice.

★ ★ ★

On September 11, 2001, more than 5,000 innocent mothers and fathers, brothers and sisters, sons and daughters, husbands and wives, aunts and uncles, friends, lovers, and neighbors were just living their lives on what began as an ordinary day. The day had an extraordinary and terrible ending, and those Americans lost their lives. It was the first time in U.S. history that American civilians were attacked on U.S. soil.

On December 7, 1941, 2,403 Americans died in Honolulu in an unprovoked attack by Japan, an undeclared enemy of our country. (At that time, Hawaii was not a state.)

World War I resulted in the death of 136,516 Americans, the wounding of 243,300, and 4,452 missing in action (MIA).

In World War II 405,399 Americans died, 172,218 were wounded, and 78,976 were MIA.

At the conclusion of the Korean War 36,940 Americans were dead, 92,134 were wounded, and 8,176 were MIA.

The Vietnam War came to an end with 58,202 Americans dead, 303,704 wounded, including 23,214 completely disabled, and 6,371 sustaining the loss of one limb or more. The MIA total is 2,504.

High as it is, the total number of those who died in active conflict with other nations is lower than the loss of those killed during the Civil War. Between 1861 and 1865, the Union lost 110,070 on the battlefield and 250,152 from disease or injury; the Confederacy lost 94,000 on the battlefield and 164,000 to disease or injury.

We Are Inventive and Creative

We don't know about you, but it would be hard to get through the day without Velcro®, a zipper, Post-it® notes, adhesive tape or, well, ah, toilet paper. Here are some other wonderful, clever, truly useful items developed or designed by Americans that make every day easier.

FOR THE EVERYDAY

- Duct tape
- ATM machines
- Packing tape
- Queen- and king-size mattresses (hey, it's one-third of your life!)
- Coleman stove, Sterno, and flashlights
- Waterproof materials
- Remote controls
- Instant replay
- Tape cassettes and videotapes
- Sports shoes
- PalmPilots for the sophisticated, and paper organizers for the rest of us
- Personal computers and ingenious software
- 78s, LPs, 45s, CDs, and whatever's coming down the road
- Stereos and CD players

FOR TIMES OF NEED

If you need medical attention, get it in the United States. We have the best-trained medical personnel and finest equipment anywhere. Americans have developed or improved upon:

- Hand-operated automobiles and vans
- MRIs
- Heart pumps
- Pacemakers
- Transplant technology
- EKGs
- Mammograms

FOR SAVING TIME

While we all need and want to conserve energy, it's impossible not to appreciate the ease and convenience of some electrical appliances. They do the work in minutes that once took hours, and they often do it much better. In the case of dishwashers, they may even improve our lives by destroying unhealthful bacteria.

- Washing machines and dryers
- Steam irons
- All-speed film technology from Kodak
- Polaroid cameras and instant films
- 30- and 60-minute film-developing systems
- Television

It's hard to imagine a world without American inventions. What will we think of next!

Our problems are man made, therefore they may be solved by man. No problem of human destiny is beyond human beings.

—Martin Luther King Jr.

OUR STRENGTH

Words like freedom, justice, democracy, *are not common concepts; on the contrary, they are rare. People are not born knowing what these are. It takes enormous and, above all, individual effort to arrive at the respect for other people that these words imply.*

—James Baldwin

We Have the World's
Best Infrastructure

Each day, when Americans wake up, nearly all of them have access to an indoor bathroom with a ready supply of clean, hot-and-cold running water and heat. When we want a meal, we can open an electric refrigerator and take out fresh foods to cook over a gas or electric stove. We can heat water for coffee or tea, put bread in an electric toaster, and begin each day knowing that the food, clothing, and products we want and need are being delivered to stores while we sleep; that what we no longer need can be picked up and discarded by a municipal sanitation crew; that the disease and death that human waste causes in so many places in this world are almost unheard of here because our sewage systems are well built and well managed. Most Americans do not even have to think about these things, they are givens. Yet, for too many people in this world, these very basic services are unheard of.

In a typical day, no matter where we live here in the United States, it is possible to talk on a telephone, ride in a car or bus, travel by plane or train, and listen to all kinds of radio programs, surf the Internet, and receive dozens of television channels. Our postal service and telephone and communications infrastructure—which includes underground cable and orbiting satellites—are unparalleled.

We can send and receive anything from a letter to a lathe from one end of the country to another via truck, rail, plane, or boat. We can drive through tunnels carved into mountains, on bridges crossing the smallest creek or spanning the largest bays.

How many places outside the United States can a living organ be packaged on ice in a cooler, then sent via helicopter or plane to save a dying patient? Where else but here could we have pizza or Chinese food or even a gourmet feast delivered right to our door? Where else can we order celebratory gifts or flowers sent overnight?

A well-designed and well-managed infrastructure allows a community to go beyond survival stage, to use the gift of time to think, create, build, share, and enjoy one another and the world around us. A working infrastructure allows us all to live better than previous generations and to help our friends all over the world achieve a higher standard of living.

Where We Live: The American Home

The American home: A place of safety and security, where families gather to enjoy each other's company, where an individual can find solitude. Home is the place to invite friends for celebration or recreation, a place to work, and a place where life happens. Here are just a few of the places in which we Americans live:

- Hogans
- Teepees
- Grass houses
- Pueblos
- Shaker houses
- Shingled saltboxes
- A-frames
- Log cabins
- Twentieth-century Cape Cods
- California Craftsman houses
- Sears Catalog houses (yes, ordered from the catalog and delivered in pieces)
- Brownstones
- Railroad flats
- Studios
- Cabanas
- Apartment complexes
- Townhouse developments
- Modular homes
- Double-wide trailers
- Brick-and-stone mansions
- Clapboard farmhouses

From igloos to skyscraper condos, Americans find the housing that works best for them. Most are practical and functional. For this, by the way, we can thank in part Thomas Jefferson, a father of American architecture. His magnificent home, Monticello, in Charlottesville, Virginia, is a model of ingenuity and creativity—from the development of a dumbwaiter to the placement of kitchens in the same building where people ate (a revelation at the time).

Architectural innovation never rests. Today's designers and builders have added practicality and flair to the modern American home. Even the tract house brought ingenious, low-cost construction to millions, and made it possible for many young families to buy their first home. Through the Agency of Housing and Urban Development (HUD) our federal government builds affordable housing for the chronically ill, the disabled, the indigent, and the poor elderly, and underwrites rental costs for millions more.

American Architecture

All over the country, native-born and immigrant architects have put their stamp on the way we live. The buildings that are our homes, that grace our universities and colleges, and house our public libraries and government offices reflect the eras in which they were built and a broad range of architectural styles. American architects are another source of pride. Here are some of our best, along with prime examples of their work.

Frank Lloyd Wright designed public buildings: Pfeiffer Chapel (Lakeland, Florida), the Guggenheim Museum (New York City), Marin Civic Center Building (San Rafael, California); Oak Park Unity Temple (Oak Park, Illinois), and the Johnson Wax Building (Racine, Wisconsin). Wright also designed such magnificent private homes as the Millard House (Pasadena, California), Fallingwater (Bear Run, Pennsylvania), and Taliesin West (Scottsdale, Arizona). Boston-born **Louis H. Sullivan**, often called the dean of American traditional architecture, blended simple geometric forms with symbolic ornamentation in his late-nineteenth and early-twentieth-century designs for Babson House (Riverside, Illinois), the Wainwright Building (St. Louis, Missouri), St. Paul's

Church (Cedar Rapids, Iowa), the National Farmers' Bank (Owatonna, Minnesota), and the Auditorium Building (Chicago).

Louis I. Kahn's masterly touch is on the Norman Fisher house (Philadelphia); the University Art Center (New Haven, Connecticut), the Yale Center for British Art (New Haven), the Kimbell Museum (Fort Worth, Texas), Richards Medical Center (Philadelphia), and the Salk Institute (La Jolla, California). **Philip Johnson's** own all-glass New Canaan House (New Canaan, Connecticut), set a cutting-edge modernist style that is still being emulated decades later; he also designed the New York State Theater at Lincoln Center (New York City). **Frank Gehry's** pushing-the-envelope style has inspired an entirely new vocabulary in twenty-first century architecture as seen in his Experience Music Project building (Seattle, Washington).

China-born **I. M. Pei** trained at MIT and Harvard. His unique perspective is stamped on thoroughly American buildings from the John Fitzgerald Kennedy Library (Cambridge, Massachusetts) Javits Convention Center (New York City), from the East Wing of the National Gallery (Washington, D.C.), to the Rock and Roll Hall of Fame (Cleveland, Ohio).

The bright white palate of the High Museum of Art, designed by **Richard Meier,** is the perfect backdrop for the artistic pride of Atlanta. Immigrant and native-born architects alike have changed the skyline of our cities. **Minoru Yamasaki's** World Trade Center in New York City changed that city's skyline when it opened in 1973 and again, sadly, when it fell on September 11, 2001. Great architecture has helped us to understand that where we live and work can be part of the symbiotic relationship between people and materials that make it a joy to go to work and a delight to come home.

In the late 1940s **Joseph Eichler** designed affordable housing that went beyond Levittown, incorporating simple form and easy-care maintenance that reflected the refreshing new concept of the California indoor/outdoor lifestyle. Brothers **Charles Sumner Greene** and **Henry Mather Greene** married Japanese detail with California Craftsman practicality to create an Arts and Crafts style that is as contemporary today as it was innovative decades ago. African-American architect **Paul R. Williams** brought tradition and substance to elegant homes in Beverly Hills and the Hancock Park enclave in Los Angeles. **Julia Morgan** designed the Livermore House (San Francisco), Wyntoon (near Mount Shasta, California), and Hearst Castle (San Simeon, California). **Ray and Charles Eames** not only designed homes but also furnishings like the Eames lounge chair, and molded plywood and plastic chairs and tables in use today everywhere, from schools to offices to homes.

Some architects design monuments. **Maya Lin's** Vietnam Veterans Memorial in Washington, D.C., is a profound example.

New twists on old styles, new materials and new uses for traditional ones, the building of stronger, more practical, and more beautiful shelters and monuments are all part of the energetic and vibrant work of our designers and architects, construction companies, and building firms.

Americans build for today and for the future.

Fort Knox

We can rest assured that our gold bullion, the backing for the American monetary system, is safe and secure in the U.S. Bullion Depository at Fort Knox. Built in 1936 and located about thirty miles southwest of Louisville, Kentucky, Fort Knox is the most heavily guarded treasury facility anywhere. It is constructed of 16,500 cubic feet of granite, 4,200 cubic yards of concrete, 750 tons of reinforcing steel, and 670 tons of structural steel. The bullion blocks look a little smaller than building bricks and are stacked, unwrapped, in the vault. Each 27-plus-pound brick contains about 400 troy ounces of gold, which is worth about $16,888. The vault where the gold is stored is made of steel and concrete and be entered only through a twenty-ton door accessible with a series of combinations, each known only to the individual who uses it.

Our European allies recognize the security of Fort Knox, too. During World War II, Fort Knox held Great Britain's Crown Jewels and the Magna Carta. Several occupied countries of Europe sent their gold here for safekeeping. All of these treasures were returned once the war ended. Our own greatest treasures—the original documents of the Constitution, the Articles of Confederation, and the Declaration of Independence—were stored at Fort Knox from December 26, 1941, to October 1, 1944, when they were returned to Washington, D.C., where you can view them today.

The United States owns other gold reserves, too, which are held in the Philadelphia and Denver mints, the West Point Bullion Depository, and the San Francisco Assay Office, all of which are under the jurisdiction of the U.S. Mint.

Investing in America:
Making Dreams Come True

The Securities and Exchange Commission (SEC) is the perfect example of how government and business can work together to make a positive difference.

Beginning in the 1920s, many investors were encouraged to buy stocks "on margin," putting a little down and paying the balance over time. This risky procedure resulted in default by many stockholders and terrific losses by companies unable to invest promised dollars in their products or service. One result was the great stock market crash of 1929, which was a factor in the Great Depression.

It was obvious that the investment process needed regulation to protect the public. The result was the Securities Exchange Act of 1934, which did two vital things: (1) required the sellers of stocks (brokers, dealers, exchanges) to inform the investor both about the company issuing the stock and the potential risks of buying that stock, and (2) required companies making public offerings to disclose meaningful, truthful financial and other information.

The Securities Exchange Act also led to the establishment of the SEC, which currently oversees stock exchanges, brokers and dealers, investment advisers, mutual fund organizations, and public utility holding companies. Its commission proposes new rules to address changes in the market, and it enforces existing rules and laws.

The stock market is like life, it's a gamble for everyone: company, stockbroker, and investor. Yet, we are free to invest in—and profit from—the ideas, products, and innovations that drive our economy.

Free Public Education

Our free public schools offer all children an opportunity that is only a fantasy in other countries: education regardless of gender, religion, race, national origin, economic background, or physical or mental disability.

Our public schools and their dedicated teachers rise up every day to meet the challenge of educating our children to read, write, do math, and learn to live with one another in an increasingly diversified and complex world. Our schools also offer students the opportunity to participate in sports, clubs and hobby groups, and volunteer efforts. Making this all happen are our hardworking, diligent teachers and their aides. These teachers, and our boards of education, and our school administrators, are doing their utmost to ensure that our children will make productive contributions to our great country.

Free public education: another reason to be proud to be an American.

I touch the future. I teach.

> —Christa McAuliffe
> First civilian in space

Let us think of education as the means of developing our greatest abilities, because in each of us there is a private hope and dream which, fulfilled, can be translated into benefit for everyone and greater strength for our nation.

> —John F. Kennedy

Free Public Libraries

One of the most valuable community services any town or county can offer is a free public library.

The public library is as up-to-date as our society: many offer the latest local magazines and newspapers from your city or around the country. Check out CDs and cassette tapes, videos, large-print books, and audiotapes.

Need a computer? Check out your library to search the Internet, e-mail friends, or use the computer to type a résumé or term paper.

You can fall under the spell of a novelist or poet's imagination or capture history in the making with biographies, photo books, and firsthand accounts of current events. Children can borrow books for schoolwork, for pleasure, for sharing with one another. And toddlers can participate in a story hour or enjoy a bedtime story you can read to them. You can learn how to knit, how to caulk your bathroom tile, or how to change the battery in your car.

And you can talk with one of the most valuable people you'll ever meet: your local public librarian. She can help you find the information you need: on loans and grants for colleges and technical schools; information about health, transportation, housing, or community events you'd like to attend. She and her staff can even help you learn how to use the computer!

By the way, the blind and visually impaired, the elderly, and hospitalized children would love to hear you read a story. Ask your librarian to direct you to agencies that need your gift! And, if you'd love to share the skill of reading with others who have not had the opportunity to learn, contact a literacy program in your area. Books: They open doors to the world.

The Scoville Memorial Library is the United States' oldest public library. The library collection began in 1771, when Richard Smith, owner of a local blast furnace, used community contributions to buy two hundred books in London. Patrons could borrow and return books on the third Monday of every third month. Fees were collected for damages, often for "greasing," a common occurrence during the era of candlelight, when wax sometimes dripped onto pages held too close to the candles.

On April 9, 1810, a Salisbury town meeting voted to authorize the "selectmen [to] draw upon the town treasurer for the sum of one hundred dollars" to purchase more books for the Scoville Memorial Library collection, making the library the first publicly supported free town library in the United States.

★ ★ ★

Town Halls

American democracy is truly democratic. Our citizens argue and discuss the issues constantly. And then they vote to implement their opinions. There's no better forum than a town hall or similar public meeting for expressing those opinions in a place where they can have an immediate effect on the policies we vote on.

From the fifteenth century on, European communities met in public buildings to discuss town government business and procedures. This style of opinion gathering and service management was so historically effective that town hall meetings were among the customs and traditions some of our first immigrants brought to the New World in the seventeenth and eighteenth centuries. Similar meetings remain the hallmark of small American communities today, where everything from zoning and traffic, school policy, building codes and billboard signs to municipal budgets and planning can be discussed, debated, and voted upon. Town hall meetings work best for local municipal or township government. Many New England communities still operate their local government this way to good effect.

"Town hall" has also come to mean a meeting or gathering of the community to hear speakers on current events, participate in debate and share opinions, without the obligation or application of regulations upon the community. The suggestion "Let's have a town hall" is an open invitation to discovering all sides of an issue- and to solving community problems requiring more than a casual conversation over coffee.

The Press and the Pulitzer

OUR FREE PRESS

When a crisis occurs, disaster strikes, or an election result is imminent, the public is eager to know about it. We are glued to our radios and televisions. We read the latest newspapers and magazines to learn all the details. We want to know the truth about world events and their impact on us. We ask the press to help us understand. Our news writers, commentators, and editors check facts, write quickly, and separate truth from hyperbole, attribution from rumor-based gossip or public-relations puffery—all on a deadline. It is not easy. Whom can a reporter trust? Is a news event staged or real? Does a source have a hidden agenda or is he an honest and ethical witness?

Freedom of the press is a two-way street between a questioning, probing, responsible news media and a discerning, challenging, demanding public. Both must be willing to separate the fun and stimulation of entertainment from the critical importance and reality of news and information.

A free press is a privilege and an essential part of the democratic process. It not only allows but encourages action to support what we believe is right and to correct what we believe is wrong. As long as our press is free, we can learn the facts, and make decisions based on those facts, not propaganda. The responsibility to know the difference is ours. As long as our press is free, we will be free.

THE PULITZER PRIZE

Each year, Pulitzer prizes are awarded to recipients who represent many of the qualities Americans revere: honesty, integrity, and patriotism. The prizes are named for Joseph Pulitzer, a Hungarian who came to this country in 1864, became a citizen and then a publisher of leading United States newspapers such as the New York *World*, the St. Louis *Post-Dispatch*, and many others. When he died in 1911, he left behind a journalistic empire, an endowment of $2 million to establish the Columbia School of Journalism, and funds for prizes and scholarships to reward and encourage public service, American literature, and the advancement of education.

The Pulitzer prizes are currently awarded annually for novels, plays, poetry, music, drama, and contributions to journalism and education. Hundreds of notable Americans have won Pulitzers. These are a few of the outstanding awards to newspapers for Public Service:

1918—*The New York Times* (first award), for its public service in reporting on World War I.

1926—Columbus (Ga.) *Enquirer Sun*, for its stands against lynching, the Ku Klux Klan, a law barring the teaching of evolution, and political corruption.

1938—Bismarck (N.D.) *Tribune*, for its news reports and editorials entitled "Self Help in the Dust Bowl."

1942—Los Angeles *Times*, for its successful campaign that resulted in the clarification and confirmation for all American newspapers of the right of free press as guaranteed under the Constitution.

1948—St. Louis *Post-Dispatch*, for the coverage of the Centralia, Illinois, mine disaster. As a result, important reforms in mine safety law and regulation were put into place.

1952—St. Louis *Post-Dispatch*, for its investigation into corruption at the Internal Revenue Bureau (now known as the IRS) and other governmental departments.

1958—*Arkansas Gazette* (Little Rock, Ark.), "For demonstrating the highest qualities of civic leadership, journalistic responsibility and moral courage" in its coverage of the first court-ordered attempts at school integration.

1960—Los Angeles *Times,* for its attack on narcotics traffic and the reporting of Gene Sherman, which led to both United States and Mexico working together to halt the flow of illegal drugs into the U.S.

1968—Riverside (Calif.) *Press-Enterprise,* for its exposé of judicial corruption regarding the property and estates of a Native American tribe in California.

1972—*The New York Times,* for the publication of the Pentagon Papers.

1973—*The Washington Post,* for its investigation of the Watergate case.

1990—Washington (N.C.) *Daily News,* for revealing that the city's water supply had been contaminated with carcinogens for a period of eight years.

1998—Grand Forks (N.D.) *Herald,* for its sustained and informative coverage, vividly illustrated with photographs, that helped hold its community together in the wake of flooding, a blizzard and a fire that devastated much of the city, including the newspaper plant itself.

2000—*The Washington Post,* for Katherine Boo's reports that disclosed "wretched neglect and abuse" in the city's group homes for the mentally retarded, resulting in reforms.

We are proud of our free press and the men and women who work hard to tell us the truth about our world.

OUR GOOD TIMES

The Constitution only gives people the right to pursue happiness. You have to catch it yourself.

—Benjamin Franklin

We Love Our Sports . . .
and Our Sports Heroes

Sports is an absolute passion for Americans: We root, we rally, we hoot and holler. We champion "our teams" and heap accolades on record breakers. We love college teams as much as the pros, and our passion begins early, with Pop Warner, Little League, and peewee teams of all types. We love the excitement of the game, the competition, the thrill of the win.

As in every other arena in American life, choice beckons us. We enjoy team sports such as basketball, baseball, football, hockey, and lacrosse, the agile game inherited from our Native Americans. Or we can take on individual challenges in golf, gymnastics, archery, or martial arts. We can skate on boards, on rollers, in-line, or on ice. We can race on a track by foot, by motorcycle, in a soap-box derby car, or the old-fashioned way, by horse.

Perhaps no sport captures the spirit of the United States better than surfing. Although born and bred in Hawaii, it is as much a passion in California as it is in the Islands, and all one needs is a surfboard, a mighty wave, and the right wet suit.

With water of every kind in our country, it's no wonder we love to swim, dive, snorkel, scuba, waterski, and sail. Fishing can be as dramatic as tugging a marlin from the ocean or as sedate as a balletic cast of the fly fisher's pole.

We even love sports at family gatherings and community celebrations. What's the Fourth of July without tug-of-war rope pulls, a three-legged race, or an impromptu game of tag football? We bowl. We play boccie, croquet, or miniature golf.

We can exercise on weight machines or treadmills; take classes in yoga, Pilates, or aerobics. We can make exercising a family affair with "Mommy and Me" classes to start babies on the road to having fun with movement. Schools offer our kids everything from archery to discus throwing, from wrestling to modern dance. And our city parks and recreation departments provide plenty of opportunities for athletic enjoyment long after graduation. And weather is never an issue. Rain or shine, we can play racquetball, tennis, handball, squash, or volleyball.

Almost anyone can find a sport to enjoy and excel in. And, of course, everyone needs a cheerleader, especially for:

BASKETBALL

It began in 1891 in a winter gym class at the International YMCA Training School (now Springfield College) in Springfield, Massachusetts. The rough-and-tumble sport was originally played with soccer balls and peach baskets. In the melting pot of our city parks and gyms, basketball evolved into a sport whose great players' names are synonymous with speed, grace, agility, and the finest athleticism. We applaud here a few of them:

Wilt Chamberlain	Julius Erving	Hakeem Olajuwon
Michael Jordan	Larry Bird	Bill Bradley
Oscar Robertson	Jerry West	Walt Frazier
Elgin Baylor	Kareem Abdul-Jabbar	Karl Malone
Bill Russell	Bob Cousy	Allan Houston
Earvin "Magic" Johnson	Shaquille O'Neal	Dave DeBusschere
Jerry Lucas	Rick Barry	Patrick Ewing
	Pete Marevich	Bill Walton

BASEBALL

The French-born American author Jacques Barzun wrote, "Whoever wants to know the heart and mind of America had better learn baseball." And who among us hasn't? It's our own, our national pastime, part of our summers and our youth. These are some of the legendary heroes of the diamond:

Babe Ruth	Stan Musial	Barry Bonds
Jackie Robinson	Ty Cobb	Honus Wagner
Willie Mays	Pete Rose	Bob Feller
Mickey Mantle	Cy Young	Christy Mathewson
Joe DiMaggio	Walter Johnson	Warren Spahn
Ted Williams	Sandy Koufax	Lou Gehrig
Roberto Clemente	Nolan Ryan	Satchel Paige
Hank Aaron	Bob Gibson	Rickey Henderson
Rogers Hornsby	Whitey Ford	Yogi Berra

FOOTBALL

The All-American sport, the weekend tailgater, the folklorist's entry into the American character: football. Knute Rockne, Notre Dame, and missing teeth. Cleats, shin pads, the gridiron. Grunts. Whether George Gipp from his deathbed ever said, "Win one for the Gipper" is still open for debate. But his greatness is not; nor is that of these players who, for all of us, are heroes, the stuff of myth:

Jim Brown	Ernie Nevers	Dick Butkus
Jim Thorpe	Terry Bradshaw	Rosie Grier
Johnny Unitas	Franco Harris	Don Hutsey
Gale Sayers	Jerry Rice	Bob Lilly
Joe Montana	Walter Payton	Larry Csonka
Bart Starr	Frank Tarkenton	Roger Stauback
Joe Namath	Lawrence Taylor	Frank Gifford

Are there other American sports heroes? Of course, and here are just a few of them:

IN TENNIS:

Althea Gibson	Bill Tilden	
Gussie Moran	Don Budge	
Billie Jean King	Arthur Ashe	
Jimmy Connors	Pete Sampras	
Chris Evert	Venus Williams	
Andre Agassi	Serena Williams	
John McEnroe	Tracy Austin	

IN GOLF:

Jack Nicklaus
Arnold Palmer
Ben Hogan
Tiger Woods
Babe Didrikson
   Zaharius
Bobby Jones

Sam Snead
Walter Hagen
Nancy Lopez
Patty Sheehan

IN TRACK AND FIELD:
Carl Lewis
Florence Joyner
Edwin Moses
Jackie Joyner-
   Kersee
Rafer Johnson
Bob Mathias
Glen Cunningham
Jim Ryan

IN SKATING:
Scott Hamilton
Peggy Fleming
Brian Boitano
Kristi Yamaguchi
Eric Heiden
Bonnie Blair

IN BOXING:
Muhammad Ali
Sugar Ray
   Robinson
Henry Armstrong
Jack Dempsey
Joe Louis

Willie Pep
Rocky Marciano
Joe Frazier
Mike Tyson
Floyd Patterson
Gene Tunney
Sugar Ray Leonard
George Foreman
Rocky Graziano

We'll remember, too, these All-American Olympians: Jesse Owens, Greg Louganis, Al Oerter, Bruce Jenner, Johnny Weissmuller, Mark Spitz, Wilma Rudolph, and one of the most inspiring of them all, Lance Armstrong.

And to end with them, of course, is only the beginning. Because your favorite athlete may, in fact, be your daughter on a balance beam, your son on the soccer field, a wheelchair-bound friend doing crazy eights and wheelies, or a young unknown you found riveting, amazing, and inspiring only yesterday.

The Bounties of American Food

The United States has always been blessed with bountiful harvests of a wide range of produce, not to mention meats and dairy products. Creative chefs, restaurateurs, and packagers help bring great food and ideas to the marketplace.

The back-to-organics movement is flourishing everywhere as farmers markets become a regular fixture in communities around the country and more people are opting for higher quality, fresher produce grown without pesticides. While large-scale food manufacturers continue to process food for larger shelf life, conventional supermarkets are devoting more shelf room to organic packaged foods and organic fruits and vegetables. There was a time when all food was organically grown, and we know now we can grow it that way again.

Community gardens are everywhere, and more people are growing their own vegetables and fruits. It's great exercise, it's a marvelous way to meet people and make friends, and you get to eat what you grow!

Boutique foods manufacturers are popping up everywhere, too. Barbecue sauces, salsas, olive oils, artisan breads, jams and preserves, sauces, handmade pastas, blue corn chips, and flavored vinegars and oils are available in every region of the country.

Thanks to state-of-the-art harvesting and shipping methods, we can enjoy all the foods unique to only certain states: cranberries from New England, lobsters from Maine, taro from Hawaii, chiles from the Southwest, hush puppies and hominy grits from the South; scrapple and hoagies from Philadelphia (which also makes a killer steak-and-onion sandwich); crab cakes from Maryland; Dungeness crabs from California; catfish from Mississippi; airy breakfast beignets from Louisiana; and unbeatable New York cheesecake, salami, and bagels.

You'll find the best steaks and burgers in Chicago, which competes with New York for the best true Italian-style pizzas. Drizzle your pancakes with Vermont maple syrup; scoop up Boston baked beans at your next picnic, along with that coleslaw, potato salad, and Coney Island hot dogs. And you'll love the tacos, enchiladas, and tostadas of Southern California, Arizona, New Mexico, and Texas (each different yet each delicious). Texas beef and pork are always winners, and Arkansas chickens rule the roost. Wisconsin and California have their cheese and other fine dairy products, and various Midwestern communities produce outstanding sausages and bacon.

Salmon, apples, and wine from Washington, berries and wines from Oregon are part of the bounty from the Pacific Northwest.

Our country's winemakers are exceptional in California, New York, Oregon, and other points. Milwaukee is still the kingmaker of beer, although boutique breweries are hopping everywhere. No one grows better citrus than Florida, Texas, Arizona, and California, and when day is done a little Kentucky bourbon or Tennessee sour mash bourbon can ease the weary bones.

Ice cream and sherbets were not originated here but were certainly perfected: Dreamsicles and Creamsicles, Popsicles and Drumsticks, Eskimo Pies and gourmet ice creams with just milk, eggs, butter, and sugar—*exactly* what the doctor ordered!

Popcorn is a national passion, and we flavor it with butter and salt, Cheddar cheese, cinnamon and sugar, and even cover it with globs of caramel sauce. Too much of a good thing, as Mae West once noted, is wonderful!

Halloween seems to bring out the sugarholics, and American candy makers are ready for them: candy corn, nut brittle and licorice sticks, sugar wafers, peanut clusters, caramels, nougat, chocolate and raisins, chocolate and mint, chocolate and almonds, chocolate and . . . well, you get the idea. And don't forget that American classic: the Hershey bar.

As each new ethnic group has immigrated to America, they've brought with them their specialties. Now you can taking cooking classes or buy the ingredients and make exotic favorites from the cuisines of China, Japan, Malaysia, Vietnam, England, France, Italy, Russia, Afghanistan, India, Sri Lanka, Mexico, Ethiopia, Nepal,

Spain, Central and South America, Thailand, Taiwan, Jamaica, Australia, New Zealand, and every other country imaginable. And don't forget regional American specialties: Cajun, Tex-Mex, soul food. It's fun, it's exciting, it's downright interesting, and it all tastes GREAT.

Thanksgiving has become our national feast day. The holiday menu may include turkey, goose, or ham; stuffing with celery or oysters or mushrooms or sausage or chestnuts; cranberry sauce; relishes; squash or sweet potatoes and brussels sprouts and corn; and pumpkin, pecan, or apple pie à la mode. Before we begin this bountiful meal, we offer thanks for our blessings, aware that some of our neighbors are wanting.

If you don't already give to the hungry or the homeless in your community, make a donation of money or food a part of your weekly grocery stops. Your religious community or your local government can connect you with agencies or services that can help you make a difference in a hungry person's life. Thanks to agencies like the Salvation Army, Meals on Wheels, Project Open Hand, and federal food programs, we're getting better at sharing our bounty with those in need.

All-American Animals

Americans have plenty of affection for their furred and feathered companions, and the more time we spend with them, the more we marvel at their intelligence and spirit. The following are just some of the ways our animals help us:

Before e-mail, cell phones, and telephones, the carrier pigeon used its unerring sense of direction to carry messages taped to its feet. Often, these birds carried messages that brought joy, relieved worry, and, in times of war, saved lives. Carrier pigeons are still used for communication.

Dogs have been born and bred to be hunters for centuries. They hunt birds, game, even truffles (as do pigs). More recently they have hunted down clues to finding the missing, the dangerous materials or explosives, and seek out people fleeing from the scene of a crime. Their critical sense of smell, their intelligence, and their perseverance has saved countless lives.

The Guide Dog program to train dogs for the blind is probably the most famous animals-for-people agency. They train both the dogs and the people, and the protection, direction, and affection of these dogs is priceless. Dogs are also trained to help the hearing-impaired and others who are disabled.

Animals for the bedridden or wheelchair-bound are a double blessing, for they give affection and provide service. For example, trained monkeys can pick up small utensils, answer doors and telephones, and give notice of dangerous noises.

The pony ride at the carnival is nearly impossible for some children to enjoy because of disability. However, around the country some specially trained riding teachers are participating in programs to give these children the opportunity to ride.

Pets for the elderly are good medicine for the depression, loneliness, or illness that can accompany old age. Mental health officials often quote the prescription of "five hugs a day." If you're not living with someone to hug, a pet is a very good substitute. Caring for pets has been a time-honored method of teaching children how to think about and care about beings other than themselves.

Whether it's the family dog or cat, a single goldfish in its little bowl, a gerbil running madly on its wheel, a parakeet, turtle, or lizard, pets are a reminder to us all that we living beings have a lot in common.

We Entertain the World

Americans have created great entertainments and technological innovations to enhance them. We have broken boundaries in art; our musicians and singers perform satire and biting commentary, love songs and tunes of whimsy, pop standards and classic opera. Our theater moves us, sends us home singing, or laughing, or thinking of conventions challenged.

Through community outreach programs, museum docents, and mobile entertainment, we bring art, music, dance, and theater to schools, hospitals, homes for seniors, and correctional facilities, parks, and other public places.

Many of our entertainers have been viewed by billions via satellite or by just a handful in institutions where a performer can bring a memory of freedom to a prisoner; a glimpse of possibilities for the disenfranchised.

Our producers and their angels make it all happen by investing in the dreams of artists. Television and radio producers bring us information and entertainment every day. We are proud of the theatrical and concert-producing community, museum directors and art gallery owners, parks and recreation departments, and all the organizations and individuals who bring art and entertainment to millions every year.

Here are just a few of the many great American producers, venues, writers/lyricists/composers, and performers.

THE PRODUCERS

Rocco Landesman
Joe Papp
David Merrick
David Sussman
Bill Graham
Sol Hurok
P. T. Barnum &
   James A. Bailey

THE VENUES

Broadway and Off-Broadway
   theaters
Branson, Missouri, theaters
Apollo Theatre
Carnegie Hall
Lincoln Center
L. A. Performing Arts Center
Kennedy Center
Our big city symphony halls

THE PLAYWRIGHTS

Eugene O'Neill
Tennessee Williams
Arthur Miller
Tony Kushner
Wendy Wasserstein
Clare Booth Luce
Edward Albee

Harvey Fierstein
Thornton Wilder
David Raab
Israel Horowitz
Sam Shepard
Neil Simon
David Mamet

BROADWAY COMPOSERS AND LYRICISTS

Tom Jones and Harvey Schmidt of *The Fantasticks*, the longest-running show of them all: forty years!

Meredith Willson

Jerry Herman

Stephen Sondheim

Jule Styne

Betty Comden & Adolph Green

Irving Berlin

George and Ira Gershwin

Cole Porter

Marvin Hamlisch

Richard Rodgers and Oscar Hammerstein II

BROADWAY MUSICAL STARS

Among the Broadway denizens who have acted, danced, and belted out songs to delight us are:

Bernadette Peters

Celeste Holm

Mary Martin

Robert Preston

Ethel Merman

Nathan Lane

Matthew Broderick

Rita Moreno

Chita Rivera

Gwen Verdon

Ann Reinking

Carol Channing

Pearl Bailey

Ben Vereen

Gregory Hines and Maurice Hines

Savion Glover

Donna McKechnie

Jerry Ohrbach

Alexis Smith

Lauren Bacall

Joel Grey

Liza Minnelli

Elaine Stritch

VAUDEVILLE GREATS

From the minstrel show to vaudeville, American entertainers traveled by train, bus, and their wits to hit the Orpheum Circuit and other theater chains from the early 1900s to the 1930s. They sang, danced, told jokes, directed animal performers, juggled, and prestidigitated. Many of these beloved vaudevillians segued to radio, and some to television, demonstrating that talent need not be relegated to one medium.

Jack Benny	The Marx Brothers
George Burns &	Mae West
Gracie Allen	W. C. Fields
Bill "Bojangles" Robinson	Milton Berle
Al Sheen & Ed Gallagher	Fanny Brice

RADIO GREATS

The magic of radio was, and is, how it can stimulate the imagination with sound alone. How heavy was the door to Jack Benny's "vault"? Was that one shot or two on *Gunsmoke*? How did we just know who the rotten scoundrels were on the soap operas of the day?

For pure delight today, listen to *A Prairie Home Companion* with Garrison Keillor, where he travels each week to Lake Wobegon where "all the women are strong, all the men good-looking, and all the children are above average."

The Metropolitan Opera can still be heard every Saturday during the season, or check out stations devoted to your type of music: heavy metal, oldies but goodies, rock and roll, country, pop, classical, and jazz and whatever's new this week.

Listen to all-talk radio and participate in forums that discuss local and national issues; listen to therapists, analysts, and car maintenance experts. Radio is a companion on a long trip, for the lonely night, for pure recreation or specific traffic and weather information on the commute to work.

Enjoy, and remember:

Amos 'n' Andy
Fred Allen
Fibber McGee and Molly
The Lone Ranger and Tonto
Soap Opera! *The Romance of Helen Trent* (Can a woman
    of forty find happiness? The show lasted 39 years.
    There's always hope!)
Alan Freed
Wolfman Jack

TELEVISION GREATS

Living with immediate, round-the-clock coverage of everything and anything anywhere in the world, it's hard to imagine a time when all television was live and all shows were broadcast in black and white. Now, via cable, you can have hundreds of channels and watch anything from how to cook hush puppies to a tour of magnificent tourist sites around the world.

Television captures world news with such immediacy that all who have lived through these times can remember where we were when we witnessed the coronation of Queen Elizabeth of England, the launch of *Sputnik*, Neil Armstrong's walk on the moon, the swearing in of President Eisenhower, or the assassinations of John F. Kennedy, Robert Kennedy, Medgar Evers, Martin Luther King Jr. We witnessed space missiles, the war zones around the world, and the joy of weddings, babies, graduations, and documentaries of the triumphs of our innovations in medicine, science, and technology. We had front-row seats to the best performers on earth from all points on earth.

Such access has also made us even more keenly aware of how open a society we have and how precious its rights and privileges are. We have bared our souls, shown the world our failures and embarrassments, our triumphs and highest accomplishments; our silliest moments and our most profound.

Here are some of the shows and personalities that have entertained us and the rest of the world:

The Oscars
Oprah!
Howdy Doody
Captain Kangaroo
Kukla, Fran and Ollie
American Bandstand
The Today Show

The Tonight Show
Playhouse 90
Loretta Young
Robert Young
Studio One
Kate Smith
Comedy Central

Dennis Miller
Walter Cronkite
Chet Huntley and David
    Brinkley
Edward R. Murrow
Ralph Edwards and *This Is
    Your Life!*
Omnibus
The Discovery Channel
Mister Rogers' Neighborhood
Sesame Street
Marlin Perkins and *Wild
    Kingdom*
NYPD Blue
Lassie
MTV

E! Entertainment
Hollywood Squares
Wheel of Fortune
Jeopardy!
Jackie Gleason
Audrey Meadows
Art Carney
Tony Randall and Jack Klugman
Donna Reed
Soap Operas!!! Susan Lucci
    and the rest
Rowan & Martin's Laugh-in
Milton Berle
Imogene Coca and Sid Caesar
    of *Your Show of Shows*
Alex Haley's *Roots*

Talk shows then and now, hosted by Merv Griffin,
    Mike Douglas, Virginia Graham, Montel Williams,
    Jerry Springer, Sally Jesse Raphael, Rikki Lake, and
    many others
Variety shows with Dinah Shore, Flip Wilson, Perry Como,
    Jimmy Durante, Dean Martin, Carol Burnett, and
    Ed Sullivan . . .

America Dances

If there is one word to describe American dance it's *energetic*.

COUNTRY DANCING

Throughout the American West in the nineteenth century, at hoe-downs and potlucks, at picnics and barn raisings, dancing was a vibrant part of the celebration. What we call county dancing was and is lively, the steps are simple, and the main goal is to have fun.

Square dancing is community dancing, where partners form squares and trade off back and forth in response to the caller's rhythmic instructions. It's breathtakingly fast sometimes, and you have to pay attention, but it's great exercise and a good time is guaranteed.

From these two traditions we have developed modern line dancing, country swing, and other variations. The music is still down-home simple melodies with lyrics made for loving and laughing—and it's hard to spend even a few minutes on a country-western dance floor and not come away smiling.

TAP DANCING

From the rough stomping of the untrained to the choreographed routine of early-nineteenth-century vaudevillians to the classical steps of sophisticated performers, "tap dancing" has become *the* American dance form in movies, cabaret, and theater. The taps on the shoes are akin to an instrument and the dancer's entire body an orchestra of movement. Some of America's greatest tap dancers were Bill "Bojangles" Robinson, Charles "Honi" Coles (whose partner Charles "Cholly" Atkins choreographed many of the great Motown artists of the '60s), Sandman Sims, the Nicholas Brothers (Fayard and Harold), Bunny Briggs, Teddy Hale, and Sammy Davis Jr.—all African Americans, all men, all talent. Too slowly for some, but thankfully not for all, they taught, they shared, they passed on their gifts to dancers white and black, men and women, so that from the twenties to today we can recall other fine tap dancers like Ann Miller and Eleanor Powell, the naïve charm of Ruby Keeler and Shirley Temple, the sophisticated yet athletic tap routines of Ginger Rogers and Fred Astaire, and the comic or elegant turns of Gene Kelly and Donald O'Connor. However, to see the pure perfection of tap dancing today, we can watch Gregory Hines, Savion Glover, and the legions of trained young dancers who have revived the art of tap.

CONTEMPORARY SOCIAL DANCING

Social dancing in American comes in at least two varieties: serious, for dancers who compete for world championships in the ballroom dance categories for waltzes, foxtrots, and tangos, and fun, for those of us who dance at weddings and parties.

America loves to dance! The 1800s, with elegant dress suits for men and ballgowns for women, saw grand dress balls where elegantly gowned women waltzed with tuxedoed partners.

Once the twentieth century began and the rollicking 1920s followed, Americans could dance all night to the turkey trot, kick up their heels to the black bottom or the Charleston—and women's hemlines rose to suitable new heights.

During the 1940s, with the advent of the Big Bands and "swing" jazz, dancing became even more athletic, with a gymnastic edge prevalent in jitterbugs and swing dancing. These styles are experiencing a comeback today, as twenty-somethings discover the fun of the Lindy and the sweetness of the two-step while a love ballad plays.

MODERN DANCE

What's "modern" about modern dance is its liberation from the formality and rigidity of classical ballet and its use of the undecorated dancer's form to tell a story.

Martha Graham, a mother of modern dance, brought an entirely new vocabulary to dance with her revolutionary ideas about lighting, stage design, costume, music, and of course, movement, which looked free but was as dramatically and carefully designed as any classic choreography ever had been.

Graham and her company danced for eight presidents, choreographed both political and poetic dances, and *Appalachian Spring*, her collaboration with sculptor and set designer Isamu Noguchi, was an unforgettable sensation. She was joined by **Paul Taylor** and **Merce Cunningham**, who would go on to form their own spectacular companies, and she created *Episodes* with George Balanchine. She herself last danced at the age of 76, but continued to choreograph new work for Rudolf Nureyev and Margot Fonteyn and was choreographing a new ballet for the Barcelona Olympics when she died at age 96.

Katherine Dunham revolutionized modern dance with the addition of elements from folk and ethnic choreography and was a leader in the anthropological dance movement. Dunham was the first black woman to choreograph for the Metropolitan Opera (her *Aida*). A lithe dancer, she fully mastered body movement for herself, then passed on her knowledge to others in her own company and in the major works she directed and choreographed. She was among the first black American dancers to present the new American dance to a European audience.

Alvin Ailey's American Dance Theater reflected all the wit and wisdom of African-American heritage and touched the heart of the traditional dance audience and the mass audience as well. Ailey masterfully blended modern dance, jazz, and primitive and contemporary stylings, with the discipline and foundation of classic ballet. He choreographed for American Ballet Theatre, the Harkness Ballet, and the Joffrey Ballet, and for his own memorable company. One of his star performers, Judith Jamison, a remarkably elegant and statuesque beauty whose performance in *Revelations* has never been matched, was a perfect muse for Ailey and now leads the company that bears hia name.

Among the other leaders in American dance are **Merce Cunningham**, whose incredibly dramatic and exciting choreography involve a discipline and style still revolutionary in the dance community; **Twyla Tharpe**, who has combined the elegance of ballet with the drama of modern dance in such seminal pieces as *Push Comes to Shove*; and **Eliot Feld**, who early on danced in the film *West Side Story* and went on to found Ballet Tech and revive New York City's Joyce Theater; and **Mark Morris**, whose dancers look much more like the rest of us than the sleek young dancers most often seen on stage. In 1976, following an illustrious career with the New York City Ballet, **Jacques d'Amboise**, a native New Yorker, founded the National Dance Institute to teach dance to public school children, their teachers, and the school staff, too. NDI instructs thousands of students throughout the country and about two thousand a year in New York City alone, where an annual performance is given on a professional stage.

BROADWAY AND THE MUSICAL COMEDY

What would a Broadway musical be without song *and* dance? The early musicals of the twentieth century reflected the style of vaudeville and English music hall dancing. It took the genius of

Agnes de Mille to break through the song-and-patter style to make dance a character, a part of the story, an integral, seamless part of the production—which she did with *Oklahoma!* and *Carousel* for Richard Rodgers and Oscar Hammerstein, along with *Paint Your Wagon*, *Brigadoon*, *Gentlemen Prefer Blondes*, and many individual ballets choreographed during the 1960s. Breakthroughs were not new to her: She was the first to use black dancers in the American Ballet Theatre, and her highly energetic *Rodeo* for the visiting Ballet Russe de Monte Carlo was called "as American as Mark Twain."

Jerome Robbins, a former New York City ballet dancer, turned choreographer for a remarkably prolific career designing performances for ballets and Broadway shows, including *On the Town*, *High Button Shoes*, *The Pajama Game*, *Peter Pan*, *Gypsy*, *Fiddler on the Roof*, and *West Side Story*. Robbins also had a prolific career in television, Broadway, theater, and with American Ballet Theatre and the New York City Ballet—for which he served as ballet master in chief.

Bob Fosse, whose precise and totally unorthodox movements dazzled audiences of *Damn Yankees*, *Sweet Charity*, *Cabaret*, *Chicago*, and *All That Jazz*, brought a sharp sexiness and hip attitude to theatrical dance. His patented and immediately recognizable shoulder shrugs, tricks with hats, outstretched hands, finger snapping, and sharp kicks have influenced dancers and choreographers from Debbie Allen to the singers and stars of today's MTV, music video, and pop concert performers.

American Popular Music

Music makes the people come together.

—Madonna

American popular music evolved from traditional music from around the world. Every style has roots going back centuries, to other places and cultures: the European folk songs that gave rise to early country music; the African traditions underlying the blues, gospel, soul, rock, and jazz; the conventions of musical composition and poetry that inform America's classic popular catalog and Broadway. Stylistic crossover has defined American popular music from the beginning, bringing the past into the present and forging unique alliances, such as the blues-country hybrid rock and roll or the soul, jazz, spoken-word blend known as rap.

Bob Dylan and Bruce Springsteen learned from Woody Guthrie; Stephen Sondheim from Oscar Hammerstein II; Billy Joel from Phil Spector and Ira Gershwin; Emmylou Harris from Gram Parsons and the Carter Family; Tupac Shakur from Gil Scott-

Heron; Destiny's Child from the Supremes. And the hits keep comin'.

THE EVOLUTION OF THE
POPULAR SONG

The American popular song has come a long way from the sweet innocence of Stephen Foster ("Beautiful Dreamer") E. Y. Harburg and Harold Arlen ("Over the Rainbow"), and Vincent Youmans amd Irving Caesar ("Tea for Two"). We were happy to sing of sweethearts, trains, April in Paris, and the good old summertime. Times change, but great songs are timeless.

In the end, however, it's love that makes the world—and the records—go 'round. Johnny Mathis, Frank Sinatra, Bing Crosby, Tony Bennett, Lena Horne, Rosemary Clooney, Nat "King" Cole, and others reinvent and revive the classic love songs, from Cole Porter's "I've Got You Under My Skin" to Billy Joel's "Just the Way You Are."

Our great songwriters include Betty Comden and Adolph Green, Dorothy Fields, David Frishberg, Frank Loesser, Hoagy Carmichael, Johnny Mercer, Sammy Cahn, Cole Porter, Ira Gershwin, Jule Styne, Jerry Herman, Stephen Sondheim, Burt Bacharach and Hal David, Alan and Marilyn Bergman, James Taylor, Randy Newman, Leonard Cohen, Smokey Robinson, Carly Simon, Carole King, Jerry Leiber and Mike Stoller, Paul Simon, Phil Spector, Doc Pomus, Neil Diamond, Stevie Wonder, Loretta Lynn, Hank

Williams, Dolly Parton, Jimmy Webb, Paul Williams, Nicholas Ashford and Valerie Simpson, Willie Nelson, and so many others.

FOLK MUSIC

American folk music began as immigrants kept alive the songs of their ancestors from around the world. During the mid–twentieth century, American folk music became more popular, thanks to the Weavers, Burl Ives, and the aforementioned Woody Guthrie, whose "This Land Is Your Land" is our second, albeit unofficial, national anthem. During the turbulent 1960s, contemporary folk music became more political, as Pete Seeger, Phil Ochs, Peter, Paul and Mary, Tom Paxton, Leonard Cohen, Joan Baez, Bob Dylan, and others voiced a nation's questions. This bold stance would be carried over into rock, soul, and country as well, expressed in songs ranging from Marvin Gaye's "What's Going On" to Johnny Paycheck's "Take This Job and Shove It."

This was not a new role for folk. After two world wars and the Great Depression, Americans discovered their vulnerability and expressed this fragility in song. Billie Holiday sang not only of the usual heartbreak, but also of lynching ("Strange Fruit") and suicide ("Gloomy Sunday"). Oscar Hammerstein II wrote about prejudice that was "carefully taught," and risked closure of his *South Pacific* when backers wanted the words stricken from the song. Hammerstein stood fast, as he did when he and Jerome Kern wrote about miscegenation and the life of Southern blacks in *Show Boat*.

ROCK

Today's popular musicians work in an ever-proliferating number of genres and hybrids: heavy metal, rap, techno, alternative country, fusion, New Age, you name it. The newest American genre—rap—recycles samples of everything from '60s cartoon soundtracks to hard-rock classics into music that is experimental, innovative, and at times more controversial than anything that's come before it. Considered a fleeting inner-city fad in the late 1970s, rap has grown from the feel-good party raps of the Sugar Hill Gang's "Rapper's Delight" to Public Enemy's militant "Fight the Power." Country music has continued to spread beyond its roots, and rock and roll keeps being reinvented. Jazz also has a growing audience among rock fans. In the end, though, rock and roll is here to stay. Here are some reasons why:

Bruce Springsteen	Carlos Santana	Smokey Robinson
Nirvana	Curtis Mayfield	The Ramones
Bonnie Raitt	The Velvet	Neil Young
Aerosmith	Underground	Big Joe Turner
Bo Diddley	Michael Jackson	Muddy Waters
Beck	Steely Dan	Wilson Pickett
Buddy Holly	Madonna	Barry White
Fats Domino	Richie Valens	Mariah Carey
The Everly Brothers	Ice-T	Jimi Hendrix
Sam Cooke	John Fogerty	Sam and Dave
Missy Elliott	Les Paul	Van Halen

Whitney Houston
Donna Summer
Etta James
The Dave Matthews Band
Sly and the Family Stone
Dinah Washington
Prince
Duane Eddy
Sean "Puffy" Combs
Jackie Wilson
Carl Perkins
The Beastie Boys
Roy Orbison
Bill Haley

Marvin Gaye
Hank Ballard
Frank Zappa
Janis Joplin
Tom Petty
Martha and the Vandellas
Al Green
Bobby Darin
R.E.M.
Stevie Ray Vaughan
Eddie Cochran
The Eagles
Otis Redding
Bessie Smith
Run-D.M.C.

Jefferson Airplane
The Shirelles
Patti Smith
The Grateful Dead
George Clinton
Gladys Knight and the Pips
The Four Tops
The Four Seasons
Elvis Presley
The Platters
The Coasters
The Temptations
The Ink Spots
L.L. Cool J
Earth, Wind and Fire

JAZZ

Perhaps no musical form says *American* to the world better than jazz. From its beginnings in the syncopated rhythms of ragtime and Dixieland to the innovations of Louis Armstrong, on through to Dizzy Gillespie, Charlie Parker, Miles Davis, Herbie Hancock, Jerry Mulligan, Ornette Coleman, Stan Getz, and Wynton Marsalis, jazz is purely original.

From the seminal *Porgy and Bess* to Dave Brubeck's "Take Five," jazz is fresh. Benny Goodman was the first to hire black and white musicians together in a band, and Wynton Marsalis was the first American composer to win the Pulitzer Prize for a jazz composition. Jazz is elegant in the hands of Duke Ellington, Count Basie, Carmen McRae, and the Modern Jazz Quartet; jumpin' with Ella Fitzgerald, Sarah Vaughan, Mel Torme, and Joe Williams; challenging in the work of Shirley Horn, Charles Mingus, and Mose Allison. It's hot, it's cool, it's smart.

AND A LITTLE COUNTRY

Country music is the sound of America between the coasts, beyond the outskirts of the big city. Although its roots lie in the folk song and the minstrel ballad from England, country music has always been consistently "popular," reaching a loyal, wide, and ever-growing audience. Here are some of the artists who make country America's music:

Jimmie Rodgers	Gram Parsons
The Carter Family	Emmylou Harris
Johnny Cash	Dwight Yoakam
Buck Owens	The Judds
Garth Brooks	Willie Nelson
Patsy Cline	Roy Acuff
Loretta Lynn	Chet Atkins
George Jones	Dolly Parton
Tammy Wynette	Bob Wills
The Dixie Chicks	Lyle Lovett

In the swift whirl of time music is a constant, reminding us of what we were and of that toward which we apsire. Art thou troubled? Music will not only calm, it will ennoble thee."

—Ralph Ellison

America Writes and Rhymes . . .
(or doesn't)

Americans love to read, and our authors are another source of immense pride. They mirror for us our daily lives, loves, and conflicts. Here are some who have written memorable works that define who we are. There are many, many others.

Dorothy Parker
E. B. White
Toni Morrison
Herman Melville
Henry David Thoreau
Ralph Waldo
   Emerson
Thomas Wolfe
John Cheever
John Updike
Norman Mailer
Flannery O'Connor
Carson McCullers

Willa Cather
Eudora Welty
Henry James
F. Scott Fitzgerald
William Faulkner
Jean Stafford
Gore Vidal
Sherman Alexie
Maxine Hong
   Kingston
Bret Harte
Nathaniel Hawthorne
John Steinbeck

Bobbie Ann Mason
Ernest Hemingway
Gertrude Stein
Pearl S. Buck
Djuna Barnes
Raymond Carver
Stephen King
Scott Turow
Tom Clancy
William H. Gass
Saul Bellow
Ernest J. Gaines
Isaac Bashevis Singer

Zane Grey
Lillian Hellman
Edith Wharton
John Hersey
James Michener
Richard Ford
Tobias Wolff
Andre Dubus
Jane Bowles
Paul Bowles

Jack Kerouac
Raymond Chandler
Ross MacDonald
Philip K. Dick
Isaac Asimov
Grace Paley
Charlotte Perkins
    Gilman
Philip Roth
Zora Neal Hurston

James Thurber
Kurt Vonnegut
Joseph Heller
John Dos Passos
Tom Wolfe
Maya Angelou
Truman Capote
Amy Tan
Ralph Ellison
James Baldwin

★ ★ ★

The woods are lovely, dark and deep,
But I have promises to keep,
And miles to go before I sleep,
And miles to go before I sleep.

—Robert Frost, from "Stopping by Woods
on a Snowy Evening," 1923

Poetry has become increasingly popular throughout our country. Poems can be soulful, sorrowful, romantic, whimsical, or hilariously funny. Here are just some American poets we're proud of, poets who have used the economies of the form in rhyme or the liberated art of free verse to inspire and thrill us, calm us, and make us laugh. Read a poem by one of these American poets today:

Philip Levine
Donald Hall
Walt Whitman
Gerald Stern
Emily Dickinson
Wallace Stevens
William Carlos
    Williams
Edgar Allan Poe
Henry Wadsworth
    Longfellow
W. H. Auden
Marianne Moore
Robert Frost
Joyce Kilmer
Stanley Kunitz
Hayden Carruth
Randall Jarrell
John Ashbery

Lawrence Ferlinghetti
Allen Ginsberg
Gary Snyder
Denise Levertov
Diane Wakoski
Gwendolyn Brooks
Lucille Clifton
Cornelius Eady
Jane Kenyon
James Dickey
Marie Ponsot
Robert Frost
Billy Collins
Anne Sexton
Ogden Nash
Sylvia Plath
Edna St. Vincent
    Millay
Donald Justice

Theodore Roethke
Maxine Kumin
Andrienne Rich
Rita Dove
Nikki Giovanni
Langston Hughes
e.e. cummings
Stephen Crane
Carl Sandburg
W. S. Merwin
W. D. Snodgrass
Paul Laurence
    Dunbar
Elizabeth Bishop
Howard Nemerov
Kenneth Koch
James Merrill
Mark Strand
Richard Wilbur

America Paints and Sculpts

American art reflects the scope of curiosity, passion, beauty, amusement, irony, and divergent points of view that can be found here. It's an art that sings with abstractions of color and the essence of narrative; it soothes, enflames, entertains, and illuminates. It can be coolly classical or wildly unconventional, yet it is always the free expression of its creators. Here are just a few of the artists who make us proud:

Mary Cassatt
Jackson Pollock
Helen Frankenthaler
Andy Warhol
Norman Rockwell
Judy Chicago
Mark Rothko
Lee Krasner
Andrew Wyeth
N. C. Wyeth
Georgia O'Keeffe

Edward Hopper
Thomas Hart Benton
Man Ray
Keith Haring
Richard Diebenkorn
Albert Pinkham
   Ryder
Dong Kingman
LeRoy Neiman
Grandma Moses
Jacob Lawrence

John Singer Sargent
Robert Rauschenberg
Willem de Kooning
Red Grooms
Maxfield Parrish
Winslow Homer
Grant Wood
Peter Max
Jasper Johns
Frank Stella
Thomas Eakins

Wayne Thiebaud
Childe Hassam
Ellsworth Kelly
Cy Twombly

Saul Steinberg
Julian Schnabel
Larry Rivers
Jean-Michel Basquiat

Alice Neel
William Merritt
  Chase
Roy Lichtenstein

Sculpting is an arduous and physical art, bringing about something magnificent from a mass of wood, clay, granite, stone, or marble. It takes craftsmanship, artistic expression, and often a very steady hand. Creating statues of monumental size also require technical prowess and the production help of many laborers. From the ubiquitous image of the sculptured heads of the four presidents on the side of Mount Rushmore to the detailed friezes and reliefs adorning many of our public buildings, the works housed in our museums and open public spaces, the art of the American sculptor is powerful to behold. We are proud of these masters:

Rudolph Evans
Vinnie Ream Hoxie
Frederic Remington
Charles M. Russell
Dale Chilhuly
Alexander Calder
Louise Nevelson
Paul Manship

Malvina Hoffman
Jo Davidson
Augustus St. Gaudens
Jenny Holzer
Robert Irwin
David Smith
Isamu Noguchi
George Segal

Theodore Roszak
Claes Oldenburg
Richard Lippold
Gutzon Borglum
Richard Serra
Martin Puryear
Betye Saar
Daniel Chester French

America Takes Pictures

The Civil War was the first military conflict ever to be photographed. The best-known photographer of this era was Mathew B. Brady. His daguerrotypes and other printed images of the people, places, and events of the war have endured as testaments to his art and to the curatorial skills of those who understood the power and importance of then-new medium of photography.

In the early 1920s, a group of creative artists made their goal of capturing lighted images on print, and in doing so, they made us look again at the simple: vegetables, flowers, and the grace of the human form. Among the leaders were **Imogen Cunningham**, **Edward Weston**, **Willard Van Dyke**, **Edward Steichen**, and **Alma Lavenson.**

During World War II, **Alfred Eisenstaedt** took photojournalism to a new level with wit, candor, and a few staged shots. His most memorable image is the sailor kissing a nurse ardently as Times Square erupts in a victory celebration. The war also brought the riveting images captured by photojournalists into our magazines and newspapers, capped perhaps by the era of *Life* magazine's star photographers, among them **Gordon Parks**, **W. Eugene Smith**, and **Margaret Bourke-White**.

From the revolutions in equipment and technique of the early 1900s to today's innovations—including digital photography and graphic reproduction—photography provides a permanent depiction of how we live. In the hands of photography's masters, American style, humor, and sentiment has been recorded for all eyes and for all time. Who can forget the Depression-era images of **Dorothea Lange**, the WPA photos of **Eudora Welty**, or the magnificence of our national parks captured by **Ansel Adams**. **Alfred Stieglitz** proved that photography is not just a record of the moment, but can be an that transform us from the indifferent to the impassioned.

Diane Arbus brought both dignity and a discomforting feeling of voyeurism to her art, as **Irving Penn**, **Herb Ritts**, and **Richard Avedon** brought elegance and grand style to the depiction of contemporary life in fashion, art, and film. And we must mention here, too, **Weegee (Arthur Fellig)**, **Gertrude Kasebier**, **Edward S. Curtis**, **Julia Cameron**, **David Douglas Duncan**, **Walker Evans**, **Robert Mapplethorpe**, **Nan Goldin**, **Mary Ellen Mark**, and **Annie Leibovitz**. They are among the hundreds of other American lensmen and women who have shocked, amazed, and brought to our attention both the harshness and the beauty of real life.

Lights, Camera, Action!

From D. W. Griffith's *Intolerance* to Irving Reis's *All My Sons* to Elia Kazan's *A Face in the Crowd*, American filmmakers have had the courage and the freedom to ask the hard questions about character, ethics, and choices. Our filmmakers have turned many a mirror to the face of injustice, and on some rare occasions raised our consciousness. Our screenwriters weave tales of love and romance, mystery and suspense, science fiction and fantasy, horror and humor. The American film industry has produced thousands of wonderful movies that entertain and inform, make us weep, laugh, and cheer.

By distributing our films around the world, we have exported American dreams, ideas, and hopes to the four corners of the globe.

Add your favorites to the following list of some American movies we love to watch over and over again.

GONE WITH THE WIND (1939)

Margaret Mitchell's long novel has it all: romance, satire, contrivance, and a surprisingly strong antiwar speech by the handsome Rhett Butler, who did, indeed, give a damn about that very uncivil war.

THE WIZARD OF OZ (1939)

Judy Garland's Dorothy takes an unexpected journey where she meets a scarecrow who needs a brain, a cowardly lion who needs some nerve, and a tin man who needs a heart. Is this political polemic masquerading as a children's story or just a tale to convince children there's no place like home?

ON THE WATERFRONT (1954)

Marlon Brando's portrayal of a New York City longshoreman who "coulda been a contender" earned him an Oscar. His onscreen rebellion against his brother (Rod Steiger) and the corrupt longshoremen's union captured the perils of nonconformity in early-1950s America.

SINGIN' IN THE RAIN (1952)

This movie within a movie is the video to rent when you want to escape. There's singing, dancing, romance, and Gene Kelly's tap splash in a puddle on an MGM backlot. Kelly, Donald O'Connor, and Debbie Reynolds make *everything* look so easy!

THE GRAPES OF WRATH (1940)

This version of author John Steinbeck's novel is an inspiring depiction of the American spirit as embodied in poor Oklahoma farmers driven west from the dust bowl during the Depression.

SHOW BOAT (1951)

Show Boat featured the unforgettable song "Ol' Man River" and starred Howard Keel, Ava Gardner, and Helen Morgan. It toppled stereotypes and showcased literacy and humanity with brilliant music by Jerome Kern and moving lyrics by Oscar Hammerstein II.

MR. SMITH GOES TO WASHINGTON (1939)

Many of us were introduced to the practice of the filibuster in this Frank Capra valentine to James Stewart's idealistic young senator who takes on a powerful Washington, D.C., political machine. It's a fantasy, but it works.

HIGH NOON (1952)

Retiring sheriff Gary Cooper is about to marry Grace Kelly when an old enemy comes back to square things up. The townspeople turn their backs on him, his fiancée holds steadfast to her Quaker belief in nonviolence, and the clock ticks slowly, determinedly toward noon. Told in real time, this is a film for today if there ever was one.

TO KILL A MOCKINGBIRD (1962)

Harper Lee only wrote one novel, but she knew when you do it right, once is enough. Gregory Peck's thoughtful Southern lawyer takes on the case of a black man wrongly accused of raping a white woman. He shows not only the depth of his conscience and high regard for the law but also demonstrates to his children the meaning of compassion. This movie is a bold and provocative argument against the evils of racial prejudice. Horton Foote's screenplay couldn't have been better.

IT HAPPENED ONE NIGHT (1934)

Clark Gable takes off his shirt to reveal he has no undershirt and the men's underwear industry takes a dive. That's the only downfall in this Frank Capra love story between a runway heiress (Claudette Colbert) and an unemployed newspaperman who smells a good story. The movie has been remade several times, but nobody did it better than this. It's fun, funny, and sweet.

THE BEST YEARS OF OUR LIVES (1946)

William Wyler's moving examination of the life of several World War II vets is propaganda at its most purposeful. A sensitive, understanding depiction of the toll war extracts on bodies and souls. It's worth it just to relive the scene of Myrna Loy's realization that husband Fredric March is finally home again. Actor Harold Russell—who was a veteran who did lose his hands—earned two Oscars, one for acting and one for inspiration.

WEST SIDE STORY (1961)

Take a play from Shakespeare (*Romeo and Juliet,*) set it in the streets of late 1950s New York, add intrinsically "American music" by

Leonard Bernstein, believable lyrics by Stephen Sondheim, and choreography by Jerome Robbins and you get 1961's Best Picture, a classic.

BUTCH CASSIDY AND THE SUNDANCE KID (1969)

We Americans love our folk heroes and our rogue outlaws, too, despite their dastardly deeds. When a movie shows them as handsome as Paul Newman and Robert Redford, what's not to love? Fun and full of action and lively wit, with a moral tale or two besides.

SNOW WHITE AND THE SEVEN DWARFS (1937)

It was 1937, and animation was still relegated for the most part to shorts. Walt Disney took this classic fairy tale, added fluid artwork, lilting songs, and marvelous voices to the world's first feature-length animated film.

M*A*S*H (1970)

This is the Robert Altman movie that spawned the television show that lasted longer than the war in Korea that it depicted. Is there a message here? Donald Sutherland, Sally Kellerman, Elliott Gould, Robert Duvall, and others push the envelopes of good taste and reverence. The result is thought-provoking and funny.

NETWORK (1976)

Paddy Chayefsky's monumental satire of U.S. network news before CNN and Fox. Peter Finch's anchor echoes the sentiment of us all at some time or another, "I'm mad as hell, and I'm not going to take it anymore!" Faye Dunaway's aggressive producer and William Holden's newsman pretend to adhere to a moral code in portrayals barely fictional, making this story as timeless as it is satiric.

THE FRENCH CONNECTION (1971)

Gene Hackman's "Popeye" Doyle is a clever New York City detective, but can he outsmart a heroin-smuggling operation and the fast-moving trains carrying the bad guys this way and that? A five-Oscar-winning masterpiece of editing, brisk direction, and clever storytelling.

ROCKY (1976)

When Sylvester Stallone's Rocky Balboa raises his arms triumphantly on the concrete steps in Philadelphia and imagines himself the heavyweight champion of the world, we root for him and for ourselves. From Rocky's American-flag boxing trunks to his modest, determined spirit, this movie all but shouts "Yes! We can!"

DUCK SOUP (1933)

The Depression-era classic that pokes fun at stuffy matrons, politics, and the absurdity of war. Groucho was never wittier, and

Harpo is literally the mirror image of himself. Black and white and all too brief.

PATTON (1970)

George C. Scott was born to play General George Patton if only to walk up the steps in the opening shot and deliver that speech with the American flag behind him. This seven-Oscar winner vividly portrays an Amercan icon.

A RAISIN IN THE SUN (1961)

Buying a home is part of the American dream, but for this black family in 1950s Chicago the dream threatens to dissolve under the weight of prejudice and interfamily conflicts. Sidney Poitier is dynamic in this challenging version of Lorraine Hansberry's play.

THE APARTMENT (1960)

Your boss asks you to do something that seems ethically iffy—what should you do? If the boss is Fred MacMurray set to have a fling with elevator operator Shirley MacLaine, he asks wide-eyed and innocent Jack Lemmon for the key to his apartment. With deft humor, director Billy Wilder turns the tables on each character and demonstrates with humor that love and affection can heal.

THE RIGHT STUFF (1983)

Many of our space heroes appear in this devastatingly thrilling and poignant look at some of the highs and lows of the U.S. space program. Based on Tom Wolfe's best-selling book, the film captured the real-life heroes—from Chuck Yeager, who broke the sound barrier, to the *Mercury* 7 astronauts. Portraying these Americans, who all have "the right stuff," are Sam Shepard, Scott Glenn, Ed Harris, and Dennis Quaid—they have never acted better.

TWELVE ANGRY MEN (1957)

Adapted from a stage play, this static black-and-white film irrevocably unfolds into a shattering yet redeeming story of twelve men, eager to judge a Spanish-American accused of murder. The lone dissenter, played by Henry Fonda, guides the others, played by a stellar cast, including Jack Klugman, E. G. Marshall, Jack Warden, Martin Balsam, Ed Begley, and Lee J. Cobb, to the realization that personal emotions and prejudice must have no bearing; only the facts of the case are at issue. Reginald Rose's script is perfect.

THE GODFATHER (1972)

Why do Americans love this cinematic saga so much? Perhaps one answer is that no matter what business these characters are really in, no matter what they do that's criminal or even absurd, they're family. Francis Ford Coppola's film stars Al Pacino, Marlon Brando, James Caan, Robert Duvall, and Diane Keaton.

And don't forget these winners, more movies we can be proud of:

Citizen Kane
Stagecoach
E.T. the Extra-terrestrial
The Shawshank Redemption
The Dirty Dozen
Friendly Persuasion
Indiana Jones and the Raiders of the Lost Ark
Star Wars
Stalag 17
Some Like It Hot
Yankee Doodle Dandy
The Sound of Music
Coalminer's Daughter
Unforgiven
Rebel Without a Cause
Casablanca
Roman Holiday
Top Hat
The Searchers
A Star Is Born
The Man Who Shot Liberty Valance
My Little Chickadee
It's a Wonderful Life
Miracle on Thirty-fourth Street
The Manchurian Candidate

Saving Private Ryan
Requiem for a Heavyweight
Fargo
The Big Sleep
Cool Hand Luke
The Graduate
The African Queen
Glory
The Shining
Vertigo
North by Northwest
Rear Window
Apocalypse Now
Raging Bull
Charade
This Is Spinal Tap
Annie Hall
Sunset Boulevard
Jaws
Chinatown
Bonnie and Clyde
The Third Man
National Velvet
The Big Chill
Fantasia
Modern Times
City Lights

America Loves to Have Fun

Americans love their toys, games, and silly gifts. Who else but an American would name a stuffed bear Teddy after a president? Who else would create the endless fun of a coiled wire called Slinky or a toy we can play with pet dogs—the Frisbee.

We love stinky, squishy, slimy things, especially in electric chartreuse or hot pink. We love our flipbooks and baseball cards. We had the whole country wiggling its hips with the Hula Hoop, talking to their pet rocks, and walking their invisible dogs on rigid leashes.

We love to play games, from charades to Trivial Pursuit, with our families or friends. Scrabble challenges the memory and the luck, especially if you get a *Q* but no *U*. And, anyone can reverse severe financial losses in the greatest board game of all, Monopoly!

Ask any American about his favorite toys, games, or treasured silly gifts, and one of these is bound to be on his list, even in an age that sometimes seems dominated by the beeping and squeaking of video games. Tonight, turn off the television and bring out the family games—just for the fun of it.

America loves to play with these:

Cast-iron moveable banks
    and toys
Lincoln Logs
Play-Doh
Jump ropes (two are best!)
Hopscotch
Pez containers
Waterguns
Jack-in-the-box
Toy pianos and xylophones
Hide-and-seek
Rubik's Cube
Old Maid and Crazy 8s
Clue, Cootie, Trivial Pursuit
Dolls, dolls, dolls—from
    Raggedy Ann and
    Raggedy Andy to Ken and
    Barbie, with Cabbage
    Patch in between

Dollhouses, too
Silly Putty
Radio Flyer wagons
G.I. Joe
Twister
Crayolas
Finger paints
Stickers! Stickers! Stickers!
Jacks
Marbles
Tinkertoys, Erector Sets, and
    pickup sticks
Lionel toy trains
Paddleball
Etch-A-Sketch

WE WILL CONTINUE . . .

I do not look upon these United States as a finished product. We are still in the making.

—Franklin D. Roosevelt

"We Will Choose Life"

"Peace Without Conquest," the address from which this excerpt is extracted, was delivered by Lyndon Baines Johnson at Johns Hopkins University on April 7, 1965. In his concluding remarks, President Johnson said:

We often say how impressive power is. But I do not find it impressive at all. The guns and the bombs, the rockets and the warships are all symbols of human failure. They are necessary symbols. They protect what we cherish. But they are witness to human folly.

A dam built across a great river is impressive.

In the countryside where I was born, and where I live, I have seen the night illuminated, and the kitchens warmed, and the homes heated, where once the cheerless night and the ceaseless cold held sway. And all this happened because electricity came to our area along the humming wires of the REA. Electrification of the countryside—yes, that, too, is impressive.

183

A rich harvest in a hungry land is impressive.

The sight of healthy children in a classroom is impressive.

These—not mighty arms—are the achievements which the American nation believes to be impressive.

And, if we are steadfast, the time may come when all other nations will also find it so.

Every night before I turn out the lights to sleep, I ask myself this question: Have I done everything that I can do to unite this country? Have I done everything I can to help unite the world, to try to bring peace and hope to all the peoples of the world? Have I done enough? Ask yourselves that question in your homes and in this hall tonight. Have we, each of us, all done all we could? Have we done enough?

We may well be living in the time foretold many years ago, when it was said: "I call heaven and earth to record this day against you, that I have set before you life and death, blessing and cursing: therefore choose life, that both thou and thy seed may live."

This generation of the world must choose: destroy or build, kill or aid, hate or understand.

We can do all these things on a scale never dreamed of before.

Well, we will choose life. In so doing, we will prevail over the enemies within man, and over the natural enemies of all mankind.

"The Americans"

In the wake of September 11, 2001, widespread news coverage was given to a remarkable editorial broadcast from Toronto by the late Gordon Sinclair, a Canadian radio commentator. What most people did not know is that Sinclair made these remarks on Canadian radio in June 1973. When released in early 1974 as a single entitled "The Americans (A Canadian's Opinion)," it became a Top 30 hit.

This Canadian thinks it is time to speak up for the Americans as the most generous and possibly the least appreciated people on all the earth.

Germany, Japan, and, to a lesser extent, Britain and Italy were lifted out of the debris of war by the Americans who poured in billions of dollars and forgave other billions in debts. None of these countries is today paying even the interest on its remaining debts to the United States.

When France was in danger of collapsing in 1956, it was the Americans who propped it up, and their reward was to be insulted and swindled on the streets of Paris. I was there. I saw it.

When earthquakes hit distant cities, it is the United States that hurries in to help. This spring, fifty-nine American communities were flattened by tornadoes. Nobody helped.

The Marshall Plan and the Truman policy pumped billions of dollars into discouraged countries. Now newspapers in those countries are writing about the decadent, warmongering Americans.

I'd like to see just one of those countries that is gloating over the erosion of the United States dollar build its own airplane. Does any other country in the world have a plane to equal the Boeing Jumbo Jet, the Lockheed Tri-Star, or the Douglas DC10? If so, why don't they fly them? Why do all the international lines except Russia fly American planes?

Why does no other land on earth even consider putting a man or woman on the moon? You talk about Japanese technocracy, and you get radios. You talk about German technocracy, and you get automobiles. You talk about American technocracy, and you find men on the moon not once, but several times—and safely home again.

You talk about scandals, and the Americans put theirs right in the store window for everybody to look at. Even their draft dodgers are not pursued and hounded. They are here on our streets, and most of them, unless they are breaking Canadian laws, are getting American dollars from Ma and Pa at home to spend here.

When the railways of France, Germany, and India were breaking down through age, it was the Americans who rebuilt them.

When the Pennsylvania Railroad and the New York Central went broke, nobody loaned them an old caboose. Both are still broke.

I can name you five thousand times when the Americans raced to the help of other people in trouble. Can you name me even one time when someone else raced to the Americans in trouble? I don't think there was outside help even during the San Francisco earthquake.

Our neighbors have faced it alone, and I'm one Canadian who is damned tired of hearing them get kicked around. They will come out of this thing with their flag high. And when they do, they are entitled to thumb their nose at the lands that are gloating over their present troubles. I hope Canada is not one of those.

Stand proud, America!

A free society is one where it is safe to be unpopular.

—Adlai Ewing Stevenson Sr.

★ ★ ★

It isn't enough to talk about peace. One must believe in it. And it isn't enough to believe in it. One must work at it.

—Eleanor Roosevelt

★ ★ ★

Democracy is not something you believe in or a place to hang your hat, but it's something you do. You participate. If you stop doing it, democracy crumbles.

—Abbie Hoffman

Freedom Is in Your Hands

Here are ways you can help to ensure freedom for your children:

* ★ Register to vote as soon as you are eligible. Vote in every election in person or by absentee ballot, but vote!
* ★ Read. Read history, read publications of opposing views, read, read, read. Teach someone else how to read.
* ★ Volunteer. Help whenever you see the need.
* ★ Get an education.
* ★ Do your job and do it well.
* ★ Protect our parks and recreation areas.
* ★ Keep recycling.
* ★ Honor and respect the freedoms and rights of *all* Americans.
* ★ Speak up against injustice.
* ★ Love your family.
* ★ Have faith.
* ★ Have fun.

Last Words . . .

Looking over our accomplishments, the people, places, things, and ideas we're most proud of, is intended to be a balm during rough times and inspiration in days of peace.

From the moment of the terrorist attack in September 2001 to these days of aftershock, we have realized that our country's principles work.

We have criticized and championed ourselves in a free press, in our right to assemble, in our freedom of speech with one another and in the community.

And we can continue.

We have prayed in the way we wish: in churches and temples, mosques and synagogues, in nature and in the privacy of our homes.

And we will continue.

We have witnessed the coming together of we the people, for the people, by the people.

We have seen firsthand what free enterprise can do to invent and create.

We know our infrastructure works. We know beyond doubt that our health, safety, and disaster personnel are trained and prepared. Our paramedics, doctors, nurses, and related medical workers are as heroic and selfless as the firefighters, police, and other Americans who protect and serve us. Our community service agencies are there to fund and support them. Our business communities and individuals of every race, creed, religion, and national origin have given their blood, their labor, and their love. And they continue to do so.

Our Founding Fathers, in their elegant legacies of rights and privileges, gave us the ultimate gift: freedom!

We *will* continue.

★ ★ ★

Acknowledgments

A book about the people, places, and things Americans can be proud about cannot be done alone. I'm proud to acknowledge the indefatigable teamwork and enthusiastic cooperation afforded me by Citadel Press director Bruce Bender, editor Margaret Wolf, and sports maven/editor Bob Schuman. Gratitude is given to the many librarians and scholars consulted, and thank you to friends William E. Johnston, Jr., Lin LaCombe, and pop musicologist Charles Wharton for eagle eyes and kind words.

DIANA ROSEN is a journalist who has written articles and books on subjects ranging from medical and psychological issues to ice cream and incense. Her book *Social Security for the Clueless* will be published by Citadel Press in 2002. She has edited the national quarterly newsletter, *Tea Talk*, since 1989 (teatalk@aol.com).

SHARE YOUR PRIDE . . .

We would love to include more people, places, and things that make America proud in our next edition. If you'd like to share, please write, in twenty-five words or less, what makes you proud about America. Send it on a POSTCARD to American Pride c/o Citadel Press, 850 Third Avenue, New York, NY 10022 or e-mail AmericanPRIDE@aol.com